# STILL WITH US

# STILL WITH US

Msenwa's Untold Story of War, Resilience and Hope

## Msenwa Oliver Mweneake

*Hope is still with us.
Arise and shine!
Peace!
Msenwa Oliver Mweneake*

Msenwa Foundation
Toronto, Ontario

Copyright © 2016 Msenwa Oliver Mweneake. All rights reserved.

Msenwa Foundation
Website: www.msenwafoundation.com
E-mail: stillwithusmemoir@gmail.com

Cover art by Heather Haynes
Cover design by Jeff Montgomery and Jarrett Montgomery

Library and Archives Canada Cataloguing in Publication

Mweneake, Msenwa Oliver, author
Still with us : Msenwa's untold story of war, resilience and hope / Msenwa Oliver Mweneake.
Issued in print and electronic formats.
ISBN 978-1-926798-52-3 (paperback) — ISBN 978-1-926798-54-7 (html)

1. Mweneake, Msenwa Oliver. 2. Congo (Democratic Republic)–History–1997– –Personal narratives. 3. Congo (Democratic Republic)–Biography. 4. Social workers–Ontario–Toronto–Biography. I. Title.

DT658.26.M84 2016    967.5103'4092    C2015-908608-6
 C2015-908609-4

# DEDICATION

*This book is gratefully dedicated to Bob and Laurie Hughes for being substitute parents when I was in desperate need. I will never forget your unconditional love and faith in me.*

*My late Grandpa Msenwa Atanda who taught me to persevere, hope and love social justice.*

*To all Nyarugusu Camp refugees who continue to struggle to barely subsist. I trust this book will solidify your trust in Almighty God and inspire hope for a better future.*

# Contents

*Praise for Still With Us* ix
*Foreword* xi
*Preface* xiii
*Acknowledgments* xv

1. Family and Communal Life 1
2. The Babembe Way 19
3. Terror on the Horizon 27
4. The Day that Changed my Life 35
5. Shadow of Death 39
6. Hope Lost 49
7. Reunited 61
8. Identity Stolen 71
9. Going Nowhere 83
10. The Daily Grind 93
11. Education: For What? 107
12. Dare to Change 119
13. Resistance 127
14. Rejection Mounting 141
15. Who Cared? 151
16. Connections 169
17. Betrayal 183

18. Distant Prospect   189
19. Patience Tested   195
20. Finding Strength   203
21. Where Am I?   213
22. Why Am I Here?   225
23. Future Gain   233
24. Hope Restored   241
25. Bittersweet   249
26. Forsaken?   257

*About the author*   262

# PRAISE FOR STILL WITH US

*As a community NGO immigration worker in Eastern Ontario assisting Afghan refugee families in the 1990s adapt to their new life in Canada, I had heard many stories from young and old about their plight in their war-torn homeland and in the camps of Pakistan. Despite previously hearing of these experiences, I could not help but be immensely moved, at times to tears, by Msenwa's story of man's inhumanity to man, and by his faith, his hope, and his ultimate desire to truly make a difference in this world.*
—Paul Kirby

*This true-life story is riveting, compelling, thought-provoking and inspiring. "Still With Us" compels us to look deep within, to examine our attitudes and reason for living. Msenwa is an example of a person who could be full of self-pity but instead chooses the road less traveled, dedicating his life to help those less fortunate. If our world had more Msenwa(s), the strife in war-torn Congo would end and greed would be no more.*
—Marilyn James, B.Sc.N., R.N

*Msenwa Oliver Mweneake bears witness to unspeakable horrors. Throughout his story it is his hope and inspiration that stand out even in the midst of year after year of hardship. His ability to sur-*

*vive is a testament to his strength and determination and allows us to see how even in the midst of such horror a human being can emerge stronger and build a full and rich life.*

>—Ellen Katz, PhD, MSW, RSW
> Director, Continuing Education
> Factor Inwentash Faculty of Social Work
> University of Toronto

*Msenwa's story shook me from the inside. He has given a voice to the millions who haven't had the opportunity to tell their own story of courage and survival. His descriptions of carefree pre-war village life makes me ache for the people of DR Congo and mourn their lost way of life. The word "Refugee" sounds and looks different to me now. This book changed me.*

>—Heather Haynes
> Artist and founder of Worlds Collide Africa

# FOREWORD

Just as Job did not take the advice of his wife to "curse God and die" when faced with horrendous adversity, the Mweneake family's fiercely held convictions have brought them through a drawn-out nightmare to the other side. Their peaceful community evaporated in an instant when marauding factions divided parents from children, exposing them to things no one should have to hear about, much less experience.

In a way, Msenwa's escape and survival story is a sort of road trip: a winding path through DR Congo, Burundi, Tanzania, Kenya and half way around the world. Like deadly games of Russian roulette, he was forced to make snap decisions that might cost his life and that of his sisters. With a bulldog's tenacity, he refused to let go of his belief that God had a plan for his life, even if that plan meant it was time to die. Not cursing God and dying, but praising God and dying.

It appears that God has other plans. Msenwa's life so far seems designed to illustrate to us in living colour what dependence on God means. From the horrific to the mundane, Msenwa's life is an exercise of living in the moment, making the choice to believe instead of doubt and to stand on the promises of God.

The lesson is not over. Much of his family continue to languish in over burdened and poorly designed refugee camps, as they have for two decades. Meanwhile, the murder and rape in his homeland continues. At this writing the world is focusing on the refugee crisis arising out of Syria and impacting Europe. If only a fraction of that attention could be focused on the ongoing misery of those suffering, not for a few weeks, but decades now, in DR Congo.

It is time for a new normal. A "normal" where indifference to suffering is unheard of, a "normal" where individuals tolerate differences and prosper in hard work, a "normal" where children are children until it is time for them to rise. That, my friends, is where Msenwa's story takes us. Like stories in the Bible, God gives us a wonderful gift in weaving a gripping story through Msenwa. It is a gift that none of us would want to live but endears us to the one who did. The world owes the Mweneake family a debt of gratitude, for it was the godly fostering of their son which has resulted in us receiving such a blessing. To share in that blessing, read on.

Paul Stevenson, PhD
Assistant Professor of Psychology
Roberts Wesleyan College
Rochester, New York

# PREFACE

This is an important book, not only for those interested in a certain period of recent Congo history but also for students and researchers in other dimensions represented in the book's content. First, the author, in his first book, gives an insider's view of the power and durability of informal education in a tightly-knit traditional village, part of a larger tribal identity. Secondly, it describes a coming-of-age story of an African child as he moves from the village, through the terrors of war to a refugee camp in another country. Throughout, the author shows his stubborn conviction, rooted in the Christian faith and in his family and tribal elders, that he is a person of worth and has a future that must be reached. Thirdly, the book documents the incredible generosity of ordinary people along the way, something that is truly remarkable — strangers who, at key points, give money, shelter, transportation, advice. Finally, the story moves into the transition from Africa to a modern industrial society, the stresses, confusion and cultural fatigue of a refugee transplanted and his eventual success. It shows the critical importance of friendly mentors for those making such transitions. The truly unusual aspect of the story is the thread of the author's amazing self-awareness at each step (and memory of it), of the emotional experiences (even anger at his parents for fleeing and leaving him and his sisters behind) and the thought processes at each challenge. There are priceless insights here for many people, involved inside or alongside, in such stories.

Gerald E Bates, PhD<br>
Chairman of Board of Directors<br>
Friends of Hope Africa University

# ACKNOWLEDGMENTS

I give glory and honour to Almighty God for His unceasing love, grace and provision throughout my life. Thank you to all the people I have met in my struggle over the years: some I have kept in touch with, others are mentioned in this book and a select few have tremendously changed the trajectory of my life. It is impossible to name all of you, but without you I would not be writing these words.

Thank you to my readers for accepting to journey and partner with me through the reading of my untold story. It is for you I have written these words.

Special thanks to my wife Miriam Mweneake for her love, encouragement and meticulous editing. I appreciate Nickie Chapman, Marilyn James, Paul Kirby and Kaede Takami for their insightful suggestions and editorial support. I am also grateful to Heather Haynes for gracing my book cover with beautiful art and Jeff Montgomery for doing the cover design and layout. I echo my sentiments to my friend Rob Clements for his invaluable support in navigating the publishing world.

I extend my wholehearted gratitude to my parents Mweniake Mwenembuka, Nam'mbongya Hegi and my seven sisters for their love and encouragement throughout my life.

Special thanks to the FreeWay Free Methodist Church for agreeing to become my sponsor, enabling me to immigrate to Canada and supporting my transition to Canadian life. I also wish to express my appreciation to Christine Flato as well as my Canadian family, Bill and Marilyn James and their children, Rachel (and husband Derek), Laura (and husband Corwin), Victoria (and husband Zach) and Julianna, for their practical love and support. Thanks to my in-laws Paul and Joanne Papps and their children, Meredith and Keenan (and wife Maria) and "Nana" Shirley Taylor, for accepting me into their family and spoiling me with their constant love.

I am indebted to my friends Paul and Carol Stevenson, as well as Weston Wachu, Philip Bahebe and Joseph Njoronge, my classmates at the University of Waterloo (MSW class of 2014) and my colleagues at the Hincks-Dellcrest Centre and the Centre Francophone de Toronto. I give special thanks to my cousins Ndanga (and family), Lucy Sikitoka, Furaha Sikitoka as well as my friends Simone Ottley and John Mukucha.

Lastly, to my anonymous educational sponsors: you have left an indelible mark on my life. Through this book, I hope that I can "pay it forward" by helping others.

# 1

# FAMILY AND COMMUNAL LIFE

---

"Éle étangaca túle nobe." *It is a miracle you are still with us.*

My Mother spoke these words to me in our native tongue of Ebembe when I was eight years old. Twenty-six years later, I can still remember those words as if they were spoken today. I can hear the words in my head and believe them in my heart, because it is a miracle I am still here, having narrowly escaped death many times under grim, dangerous and horrific circumstances.

As we walked down a dry, dusty path carved by several generations and thousands of feet, my mother told me how I was brought into the world on a hot summer evening in 1981 after a terrible pandemic had taken the life of fifty little ones in the village. My eldest sister Ne'ema (Grace in English) was spared but her sister who was born two years later, died within three days, having succumbed to tetanus and postpartum infection. The loss of this precious little daughter was an emotional wound which burdened both of my parents and triggered worry each time I contracted a life-threatening illness.

I was born in the Democratic Republic of Congo (DR Congo), the second largest country on the continent of Africa. I was born in Lusenda, a small eastern village with a population of 6,000, situated in Fizi, South Kivu province on the shores of the stunning Lake Tanganyika. The DR Congo was previously known as the Belgian Congo in colonial times and later, Zaire. It sits in the centre of Africa, surrounded by news-grabbing countries such as Uganda, Rwanda, Burundi, Tanzania, Sudan, Angola, Zambia and the Central African Republic. It is arguably best known as the setting of Joseph Conrad's book, "Heart of Darkness" and the 1974 Foreman/Ali boxing match, "Rumble in the Jungle" and unspeakable, unfathomable terror.

As a child I knew nothing of what happened outside of my village, Lusenda. I was blissfully ignorant of the world beyond, happily nurtured by my communal village-family. Lake Tanganyika, with its postcard beauty and the surrounding jungle, provided endless adventures for a child, balanced with the responsibility of helping family obtain provisions. Both were fun for a child, yet filled with dangers.

I was more fortunate than many in Lusenda because my Father had a good position as the primary school headmaster. He was also a trader, farmer and small business entrepreneur. My mother was a nurturing housewife who kept us fed and clothed. But even these two wonderful and loving parents could not keep disease away from our simple grass-roofed home, nor could they insulate us from the horrors to come.

Our rudimentary health dispensary in Lusenda, lacking in modern amenities and services, was ill-equipped to deal with serious medical issues and catastrophic disease. The sick were forced to walk hours to Nundu, which housed the only health centre in the area, serving over fifty villages and other neighbouring districts; unsurprisingly, demand was always high and patients endured seemingly endless wait times. Yet those who walked there were the lucky ones. Many families simply could not afford to take their children to the hospital and had to rely solely on traditional medicine.

About a year later, while my parents were still mourning the loss of their daughter, my Mother became pregnant with me. She told me, "You were not an easy pregnancy. I was in and out of the hospital several times with malaria, causing high fevers. I wondered if I would lose you just like your sister, but the prayers and encouragement of family and friends made all the difference."

With these words, the sad memories clouding her countenance gave way to a smile as she gently told me how she had eagerly awaited the news indicating my gender. Since ultrasound technology was not available to expectant mothers in our village, parents relied on *les sages femmes* — literally "wise women" in French, or "midwives" in English — to predict the sex of a child (French words and phrases still permeated our language — a vestige of colonial times). These wise women confidently prophesied that I would be a girl.

Finally, on the hot and muggy night of July 5, 1981, I arrived — a night that surprised many with joy and laughter as they gazed in wonder at the unexpected boy. In my culture, newborn babies are welcomed into the world through dance, song and a celebratory feast. I was no exception. Exuberant songs filled the Nundu Deaconess Hospital as family and friends celebrated my first murmurs and cries. My cousin raced about nine kilometres from the hospital to Lusenda to announce my birth. Although my parents had expected another girl, they were overjoyed to have a son they could name after my Mother's father, "Msenwa."

My Grandfather, "Msenwa" was highly respected among the Bembe people (referred to as *Babembe* or *Babondo* for plural, or *M'bembe* or *M'bondo* as individual) because of his tireless efforts helping widows, orphans and the most disadvantaged of our area. As a result of his prayer and deliverance ministry, my Grandfather became known as "Msenwa" meaning "someone from whom even demons flee." People crowded around the hospital bed where my Mother held me, swaddled in warm blankets. As they congratulated her, they inquired about my name. She confidently announced that I was named after my Grandfather, "Msenwa" to which they joyfully remarked, "He will surely be like his grandfather and continue to inspire hope in the oppressed."

Two days after my birth, over thirty women from our

village accompanied my Mother and I home to Lusenda, where hundreds of family members and friends welcomed our arrival. To celebrate my birth, a feast was prepared with a slaughtered goat and chickens, along with plentiful fish and food staples.

Two months later, unfortunately, I was back at Nundu Deaconess Hospital in the intensive care unit, suffering from malaria and a high fever. My parents knew the grim odds of survival in our area, where many children did not live past the age of five. Thankfully, with medical treatment and the prayers of many, I overcame my first battle in life.

"It is a miracle you are still with us."

Just two years later, my Mother became pregnant again and bore twins, but my new brother and sister only survived one day. My parents returned home once again with empty arms and hearts full of sadness, mourning another loss. They became very fearful I would not make it, having already lost three children.

A year later, my Mother bore a daughter, Eca (the name given to a child born after twins). The family kept growing every two years with the arrival of more sisters: Furaha and Mapenzi. Each of us was rushed to the hospital more than seven times before the age of five. My parents worried that one, if not all, might succumb to malaria or other common diseases that killed many in the village. Subsequent malaria, dysentery and stomach infections linked to unclean drinking water almost caused my demise several times over the course of my childhood.

"It is a miracle you are still with us."

Lusenda had no school program for children less than six years of age, so every morning I would watch my Father and sister go to school while I amused myself outdoors. By age five, I had mastered the art of tree climbing. As soon as my Father left the house with my sister, I would climb the *atùcu* tree outside our front door. I would swing from a branch, shouting exuberantly, "Naenda Kenya Nairobi, kuja ni kubebe? Naenda Kenya Nairobi, kuja ni kubebe?" (In English, "I'm going to Kenya Narobi, Kenya Nairobi, anyone need a ride?")

I was unaware of geography or history as a preschooler and had not been told about Nairobi, Kenya by my parents or anyone else in my village. Like everyone else, I was perplexed as to where the declaration that "I'm going to Kenya Nairobi" came from. Everyone would look at me in amazement. One elderly man in particular would often pass by and tell me, "None of your ancestors have ever been out of this village, let alone to Kenya! What is wrong with you?"

One day, Grandpa Msenwa heard me announcing my trip to Nairobi, Kenya, as I swung on the tree. He laughed as he gently brought me down from the tree and enveloped me in a warm, grandfatherly hug while saying, "I want you to know that you will one day go to a faraway country. You will be blessed to bless others and you will help many orphans and widows." As a child, I was confused by his words and simply kept swinging and singing, day after day.

When I was still a preschooler, my parents tore down their grass-roofed house and replaced it with a large brick house with an iron-sheet roof. Our new home had four bedrooms and two sitting rooms and was widely considered the best house in the village for many years. As the only boy, I had my own room while my four sisters shared one bedroom. Another bedroom was reserved for visitors and the fourth for my parents. Our house was always full of family members and visitors. When extra visitors came, we would give up our bedrooms and sleep on a mat on the cement floor. We learned that nothing belonged to us — everything was to be shared.

Lusenda had three poorly equipped primary schools and a single high school. I started primary school at age six. Soon after, I became the owner and operator of a small poultry business consisting of six hens and five roosters. The organic hens produced chickens that I would sell in August before school started in September. I used my earnings to buy school supplies.

In DR Congo, primary and secondary schools consist of six years each. After the second year of secondary school, every student has to choose a specialization (e.g. education, social studies, business, biochemistry, tailoring or agronomy) for the remaining four years. Ebembe was my mother tongue but the primary language of instruction was French. I also learned Swahili in school. As an older child, I dreamed of becoming a lawyer, fuelled by a desire to see a better DR Congo, where all Congolese would enjoy the many resources that had long been exploited by foreigners. Listening to elders and history teachers, I could not understand why bloodshed had been the only approach to resolve conflict.

Fishing and farming were the economic mainstays of our village and country and in both activities I was an active participant. Catching fish from the lake after school was not only fun but it also promised a delicious dinner and assurance that hunger pains would be abated. It was a cultural expectation to share whatever we had and it was considered rude to only offer someone food if they asked for it. Therefore, every time we went fishing, we would distribute the catch among everyone. In this way, if one person enjoyed a successful catch, the whole group benefited. Many nights, my stomach was satisfied because of someone else's catch. The game of catching and throwing away fish was unheard of and it was never an option to keep the catch to myself.

As a young child, I would swim in Lake Tanganyika, water also occupied by crocodiles, water snakes and hippopotamuses. I learned to swim quickly and get out of the water at the first sign of danger. One day as I was swimming, my friends on the shore started screaming at me to get out. I swam as fast as my little legs could propel me, not knowing what dangerous creature was nearby. Once safely on shore, I realized a crocodile had come within inches of devouring me.

"It is a miracle you are still with us."

The more I learned about dangers around me, the more I felt there had to be a higher power protecting me. Knowledge of such dangers, however, did not stop us from swimming in Lake Tanganyika — it was our only swimming option. We played many games in the water (hide and seek was my favourite) and I found it a unique place to connect with nature and the Creator.

Growing up in my village Lusenda, I quickly learned to climb mountains and all sorts of trees in search of food, a necessary skill for survival, but I had competition. Monkeys feasted on the same wild mangoes, avocados, oranges, pears and other fruit that I found so delectable. I bravely fought the monkeys for my daily portion and sometimes the monkey became my meal.

Although it would infuriate me to see a monkey dash away with my coveted pear, mango or orange, I still revelled in playing with these wild animals, for I had faith they wouldn't harm me. I treasured my walks in the jungle, discovering wild fruit and foliage that provided the necessary energy, vitamins and medicinal remedies used by my community. I never imagined that these simple joys would one day become a mere dream to all the children of DR Congo. War was looming and life in the village was about to change in traumatic and irreversible ways.

Living in a small village without electricity and a grocery store, we fully appreciated the various kinds of food each season brought. Mushroom season was my favourite. This season took place between February and April. As children, we would run home when school was dismissed in the afternoon, unload our school supplies and then invade the nearby forest in search of mushrooms. Everyone would gather buckets overflowing with mushrooms. All of us between the ages of six and thirteen knew which types of mushrooms were safe to eat and which were not.

My lucky moment came one overcast afternoon as I combed the forest for mushrooms. Fearless of poisonous snakes, I stumbled upon the biggest mushroom I had ever seen. In my mother tongue, Ebembe, this mushroom is called *taka'a*. This one was enormous and at eleven years of age, I had to call for help to pick it up. Five children joined hands to pluck the heavy mushroom from the ground. As we marched home with my prized taka'a, it began to rain. Luckily enough, the mushroom sheltered us from the gentle drizzle. I gazed up into the umbrella of the taka'a with wonder, marvelling at this creation.

Growing up in Lusenda, children learned to appreciate nature to the fullest. We lacked commercial toys, but nature provided all we needed to play: we made soccer balls from dried banana leaves and crafted many other toys from the nature that surrounded us. Some of my favourite and most memorable times were during full moons, which occurred around every twenty-eight days. On those nights, children from every corner of the village would sneak out of their homes to play hide-and-seek in the moonlight. We would spend hours scampering through the bush as we watched the luminous moon move across the sky.

Although my parents did not approve, my two sisters (Ne'ema and Eca) and I devised ways to sneak in and out of our house in order to play during the night hours. I would intentionally leave my window unlocked from the inside, but made it appear locked on the outside to prevent robbery. The window was our means to exit and enter the home without parental detection; otherwise, if caught, the next day we would be punished with a whip made from banana leaves.

Lusenda is home to many dangerous animals including deadly snakes, ninety nine percent of which are poisonous. My friends and family members were bitten on several occasions but survived with the help of Babembe traditional medicine. Every family in our village had what we called an *ibwe lya ngyo'a* in my mother tongue, literally translated as "snake stone". This stone — small, black and porous — was always in high demand as people would often get bitten by poisonous snakes. Whenever someone was bitten, they would run for this stone and apply it to the bite, believing it would draw out the venom. The snake stone reflected our culture's reliance on natural remedies, traditional medicine and customs.

I also learned that applying python oil before entering the jungle could prevent you from becoming a snake's victim. I wondered why, until my Grandmother gave me the Babembe explanation: "The python is the king of snakes. Applying its oil sends a message to other snakes that the king is close. This tradition started because people had no way of dealing with dangerous snakes. One day, a man killed a python, ate the meat and started applying its oil every time he went into the jungle."

Although not everyone believed in this practice, many people continued hunting pythons for their meat and oil to protect themselves. In addition, I learned to never whistle in the forest as it summoned the snakes. I had considered this to be superstition, until one day when my cousin Alúta and I started whistling in the bush. To our great surprise, two snakes slithered towards us and we had to jump out of the way. To this day, I still wonder why whistling beckons snakes. Although I did not fully understand all the traditions and customs of my village, I valued my culture and appreciated its practical applications.

While life seemed to be going well, I became profoundly worried about my Mother who was taken to the hospital several times in one month. As a child I did not know what was happening, except that she was pregnant. Fear paralyzed me and kept me from going to school or playing with friends. Another sister, Zawadi (meaning God's gift) was finally born after a nerve-racking pregnancy. Gazing at my Mother lying in a hospital bed, I became acutely aware that life was full of both happy and stressful moments.

My Father was not only a school Headmaster but also a farmer and businessman. To adequately provide for the family, my Father sold timber, salt, palm oil, coffee, beans and other crops we cultivated on our farm. I learned the art of farming at a young age from my Father. Both my parents highly valued education and I had the privilege of attending one of the best schools in the area. My Mother did not finish primary school before marrying my Father, but she could read and speak French and she always supported her children in their studies.

My Mother stayed home to take care of the children, making life at home lovely and safe. She made wonderful meals by mixing cassava leaves with smoked fish or meat and ground peanuts to thicken the sauce to go with *ugali* —

a delicious dish made from corn or cassava flour and water. She would also sing to us before going to bed.

Even as a young boy, my Mother would often tell me, "You won't always be with us. You need to study hard, because education can take you further than you ever imagined. I do not want you to be like me who married instead of continuing education. Although I do not regret being married, I wish my parents had encouraged me to study more." I can still clearly hear my Mother repeating over and over, "Masomo male ité até a'mbaté ikyù mena ose u'a halakwa" literally meaning "education is like the cassava tree — it can grow wherever you throw it." "No woman today," she continued, "will like a short boy like you who has no education. You better get educated, since it will add the height that you did not inherit from us."

As a child, I found it fascinating to learn the Bembe cultural roles for men and women, particularly in raising children. Fathers are the primary disciplinarians, while mothers tend to be their child's friend, confidante and advocate. My sisters and I would run to our Mother to share our secrets and she would often advocate for us when we did not follow the rules and deserved the whip, to be administered by our Father. Children are highly valued in the Bembe culture and this is reflected in large families. My parents have eight living children, including Evelyn and Nyota who were born in Nyarugusu refugee camp (plus five who died — three in DR Congo and two were miscarried in the camp).

Growing up with seven sisters and no biological brother of my own, I learned to play all sorts of games with my sisters. I also gained the stamina to walk and run long distances, in eager anticipation of the annual running and walking competitions in Lusenda and neighbouring villages. Winners would receive a basket of smoked fish, fruit and sometimes school supplies. I proudly won many times.

People in the village would make fun of me since I had only sisters. I would cry and ask my Mother why I did not have a brother. I did not understand why she cried, until years later when I learned that many in the village made fun of my parents because they had so many girls and only one boy. My mother also told me later that in the Bembe culture, boys are more valued than girls. This made me cry even more as I could not understand why people were treated differently based on gender.

My Father explained that the Bembe culture is patriarchal, a system in which the tribal lineage follows the male. As young as I was, I asked questions about how this cultural belief affected the way they treated my sisters. I came to learn that, among other disadvantages, girls would have fewer educational opportunities than boys. My Father also explained that in this patriarchal system, women cannot receive an inheritance if their parents pass away.

My parents and I would regularly discuss topics of gender, culture and tradition. Finally, one day I mustered the courage to ask my Father, "If you and Mother died today, what would happen to your farm, house and everything you have? Who would get what and why?" My Father was shocked at my questions and remained silent for a few minutes. As a young child, I was curious about my culture and did not know that death was a taboo topic — talking about it was interpreted as if I wished death to happen.

Finally, my Father broke his silence, "Remember, my son, that no culture is perfect. Every culture has rites, beliefs and customs to distinguish them from other people; however, many of these customs are based on societal assumptions that discriminate against some at the expense of others. Gender roles go far back, to the time of our forefathers. I guess the Babembe established this practice to maintain male dominance." My Mother, hearing our conversation added, "But if we die, what we own will be for all our children. We were blessed with each of you and you are all of equal value to us and the Creator."

As we discussed the issue of death, horrendous images of my two close friends flashed in my mind. Both of these friends had recently died, one of malaria and the other of cholera, both of which could have been prevented with the right treatment. Malaria, cholera, tetanus and water borne diseases at times caused the death of 4 out of 5 children in my small village. The cholera pandemic would often occur in summer, ravaging both children and grownups, spiking the mortality rate to three percent of the entire population. I remembered crying sorrowfully when my parents told me I could not attend burials because I was an eight-year-old child. "Children cannot understand these things at such a young age," they told me.

People in the village relied heavily on traditional medicine. In keeping with this emphasis, as a child, I was instructed on the medicinal properties of different trees and leaves. Our first aid kit was comprised of ingredients gathered from the forest around us. Since stomach pain was a common ailment, I learned to run to the bush, identify the helpful leaves and chew them to alleviate the pain. Everyone knew what to do for pain and sickness; it was passed on from generation to generation by word of mouth. We had no library, but had the privilege of learning firsthand through storytelling. In our oral culture, our grandparents and all elders were considered a resource and wealth of information that we could easily consult in times of need. Everyone in the community was willing to help and share their perspectives on life.

Everything revolves around relationships in the Bembe culture. There are clear expectations and guidelines on how to treat people based on their age and family position. I quickly learned that we were all connected and that is why a distant relative was also called brother, sister, uncle, aunt, mother or father, depending on the family connection. Life was just like that – relationship, relationship, relationship.

At that time, I did not fully understand what it meant to go hungry as it was acceptable to eat at anyone's house in our village. Everyone was encouraged to be generous and to help each other navigate stressful situations and persevere despite the hardship of everyday living. "You must make deep connections with your Creator, yourself and others," my parents would say. As a child I did not fully understand what this meant, but looking back now, I can see how these connections have sustained me through times of desperation and hopelessness.

Many rituals and events took place in our tiny village every year to deepen these connections, such as circumcision for boys, initiation to womanhood for girls and summer gatherings where youth were taught their ancestors' history and the struggles they endured. I can still recall my parents saying, "Pulling away from others as a way to prevent pain from occurring does not work: estranging oneself from others creates even more pain and suffering."

As a child, I did not know why it was emphasized that we don't have control over life; bad things happen to good people and because of the brokenness of human nature, life is not always fair. I quickly learned that the only thing we can control is the decision to not be defined by life's circumstances. "Whether we like it or not, traumatic events happen to us and will continue to happen," my parents said. Not knowing that one day I would become a victim of war, my parents added, "Traumatic events often disconnect people from others. However, do not forget that there is incredible curative power in our relationship with the Creator and in our ability to connect with others."

I learned another key lesson from my Father, a war survivor himself and someone whose father had died when his mother was one month pregnant with him. My Father said, "It is in the struggle that human beings are transformed to something more authentic and striking. All my success as a primary school headmaster, businessman and farmer came from my striving through hardship and deeply connecting with the Creator, people and nature." This is what would help me persevere in the midst of horrific experiences during the war that was yet to come, as a teenager responsible for my own life and that of my two younger sisters (aged six and eight at that time).

Life in my village made me strong and helped me realize that all human beings are born with the will to live and an innate desire to triumph over difficult and traumatic events. Looking back, I admire the courage of my parents and everyone in my village; they taught me to look at tragedies as a part of life and as opportunities for growth. However, little did I know that the calamity of war and misery would sorely test my resilience and sense of justice.

# 2

# THE BABEMBE WAY

Some of my most treasured childhood memories were formed under mango trees as I listened to the recounting of events about our district and country by village elders. Knowledge was transmitted to children in the form of oral stories, proverbs and songs. We were told about the hardships of our ancestors during colonial times. Listening to my elders, I fully believed the dark history of past generations was over.

The time had come to enjoy the prosperous DR Congo that I knew, walking through lush green forests, skirmishing around crocodiles in sparkling lake waters and eating delicious fruit, mushrooms, fish and wild animals. I was excited to see a Congo where our coltan, diamonds, cobalt, gold and other natural resources could be used to better our lives. Who would have predicted that within a decade this childhood assumption would be shattered?

Like many Bembe villages, Lusenda elders would gather young boys and girls at a village home to teach our culture and history. At a young age, I took great joy in learning about my individual and communal identity. There were no written documents about the Babembe or their history because knowledge was transferred orally and experts came from different villages to share their perspective on various aspects of our history.

During childhood, I loved learning new Ebembe words and proverbs. In all the gatherings, the elders would emphasize our culture's founding spiritual convictions. The Babembe believe in one God, Abeca Pùngu, Abeca Mwene-Ikùlù, Abeca Mwene-Malango, Abeca Mwene-Batù, Abeca M'mbumba Esé n'Ikùlù (God Omnipotent, God Omnipresent, God Omniscient, God the Creator of man, heaven, earth and the universe). This belief in God is a key spiritual determinant of Bembe customs and traditions.

Growing up as an M'bembe boy, I learned to hunt, fish, climb trees and farm the land. One time, I had the opportunity to dig for gold during a visit to Mienge, the natal village of my paternal grandparents. Another time, two boys and I went hunting with a fifty-year-old man. Five hours later, with no meat to show for our efforts, we stopped under a tree to regain our strength.

The elder came and sat close to us, looking deep into our eyes. "You are lucky this is not the time of King Leopold II," he said in a wavering voice. This captured our attention. We stared wide-eyed at him, eager to hear the story as he began, "Although King Leopold II had never set foot on Congolese soil, he exploited and massacred its citizens to accrue personal wealth. Everyone in the country worked tirelessly day and night to produce rubber, ivory and timber for him. Those who could not, were imprisoned or slaughtered."

That day, I caught a glimpse of the horrors of Belgian rule over the previously named Belgian Congo (1905-1960). My ancestors were used as slave labourers to plunder our own country's resources. However, I was also proud to learn that many of my ancestors had survived these atrocities and emerged to form the Bembe tribe, now known as one of the most fearless tribes in DR Congo.

Growing up in Lusenda, I gained an enhanced understanding of Bembe culture after going through the rite of passage at age eleven. There is no initiation ceremony for Babembe girls and no female genital mutilation practices; however, grandmothers, mothers and aunts are expected to initiate the girls into womanhood through storytelling at their various gatherings. Boys go through an initiation ceremony called *bùtende* (circumcision). This rite of adolescence is intended to teach them the traditional role of men.

During this rite of passage, boys between seven and sixteen years of age leave their village for three to four weeks. During this time, they are circumcised and connected with a mentor who will provide support through the rest of their life. There is joyous drumming, dancing, singing, drama and eating on the day the boys return to the village. This rite of passage taught us to be proud to be Bembe and to speak, dream and laugh in Ebembe.

A time would soon come when many were killed for

being Bembe, yet I salute the efforts of those who fought for us. We were taught that life is all about relationships and that to be Bembe is to be strong, communal and respectful of human dignity. We were also taught to defend our land and ourself until death and to be willing to stop anyone who tried to dominate or enslave us. We became fearless and willing to die for what we believed in.

As a young person, I eagerly anticipated wedding ceremonies. Goats, cows and chickens were slaughtered for the celebratory feast. A ceremony's success was measured by the number of people who came. Everyone in the village was welcome, without being sent an invitation; no one was looked at in suspicion for attending. You just showed up with an empty stomach, helped in some way, danced, sang, ate as much as you could and after, you would be given leftovers wrapped in banana leaves to take home. Before the wedding ceremony, the groom's family was expected to pay a dowry to the family of the bride. Traditionally, cows, goats, hunting tools and clothes were given in exchange for their daughter's hand in marriage.

As is the norm in many parts of Africa, families are constituted in various ways. As a youngster, I was often confused by the Babembe definition of family. Everyone was presented to me as family and had a specific title. My parents would introduce people to me in the following manner: "Son, this is your cousin, Bya'ombe. You remember meeting Ùngwa's mother. Well, this is her brother's son's youngest son." Their explanations of relationships would often puzzle me until I realized that the Babembe are not so much concerned with the genetic aspect of family but the social ties that bind people together in community. I thereafter learned from my parents that the Babembe define success as "nothing other than being able to live in relationship with others, ourselves, nature and the Creator."

The Babembe's definition of family involves several generations and all extended family, much like a clan. The extended family is a cooperative work group that shares food, gifts, money and other material items. It chooses to live in harmony with each other, with nature and to hold shared beliefs. Within this type of extended family system, grandparents, parents, sisters, uncles, aunts, cousins, nephews, nieces, church members, village residents and visitors all became part of my family.

I learned to treat anyone of my parent's age as my own parents; similarly, all elders became my grandparents. I loved to meet elders on the street and offer to carry their heavy luggage on my head; is it any wonder I am short? At times, I would even walk with them to the next village. Before leaving, they would offer a prayer or pronounce a blessing on me and send me on my way with my belly full of ugali.

I learned that it is everyone's responsibility to care for children, elders and each other. By age five, I was assisting in the care of my sisters, nieces, cousins and anyone else who needed help in the village. My Grandma would say "Mwana ale w'ebùndé" meaning "it takes a village to raise a child." All community members took responsibility for supervising and disciplining village children. Anyone who saw me misbehaving on the street acted like my own parents (or sisters) to discipline me. Particularly in Lusenda, the community played a central role in peoples' lives, providing important roles such as healer, mentor, counsellor, political and religious leader, resolver of disputes and provider of practical and emotional support.

Through everyday interactions, it became clear to me that the Babembe worldview is holistic and holds the belief that people are naturally spiritual and physical. I was amazed at how many times my people had a spiritual explanation for the world around us. Rituals and healing ceremonies were conducted regularly — nature and the Creator had everything we needed to live. Life was considered sacred and should end naturally at an old age. Death of a young person was considered a supernatural attack (witchcraft). Traditional non-Christian Babembe are petrified of death; however, many believe that the dead continue to live and that they often intervene to protect the living.

At an early age, I was taught to see the connection between health, food, work, culture, family and community. Our ancestors taught us it was essential for survival and the welfare of present and future generations to be good overseers of the land and its sustainable resources. We were also taught to live in harmony with each other, respecting leadership and providing for all.

My village members would say that our ancestors and the Creator were happy every time we obeyed these guidelines. No M'bembe would ever disobey elders, unless they wanted to be excommunicated or considered one of the *m'nyabilongo*, literally meaning "foreigner." Communal values, including respect for elders, caring for others including those with disabilities and coming together in times of crisis or difficulty, continue to be strong convictions today.

Living in Lusenda as a child was blissful; no fear or suspicion ever occurred. I was safe and cared for in my village, until I was abruptly uprooted and robbed of family and hope. Irreversible change was looming and our generation would be thrust into a period of time where we would experience unfathomable cruelty. Human greed, abuse of power, poor leadership and insanity would soon result in some of the most horrific events in modern history.

# TERROR ON THE HORIZON

"Our country has all the skills, talent and natural resources to flourish," my grandparents would emphasize, "but we have been afflicted by more than one hundred years of war. Our beloved DR Congo has suffered more atrocities than any other country on earth. Since colonial times, people have particularly abused us here in the Fizi district of eastern Congo. This has kept us in a state of chaos for many, many years." As a child, I was ignorant of the political, social and economic factors that were beckoning war closer and closer to our district. I could not imagine my generation experiencing the same suffering as my elders and ancestors. Yet the terror that would uproot me from everything familiar was just on the horizon.

War.

The rumours started in early 1990 and continued into 1993. I did not fully understand this word but I knew my parents did. I could see the fear and uncertainty in their faces as they spoke to other village members in hushed, anxious voices. I asked myself many questions in an attempt to process the rumours of war: does this mean everything that brings me joy and security will be taken away? What about my chickens? What about connecting with my people, swimming in Lake Tanganyika, mushroom picking, playing soccer, climbing trees, exploring mountains, running alongside monkeys and chimpanzees and dodging deadly snakes in the bush? All these experiences not only gave me a sense of worth and identity, it was the only life I knew. I would never trade my life as a village boy for anything. More so, living in Lusenda as a child, I never envied what others had, or thought that life could be better anywhere else. Everyone in my village was satisfied and no one had aspirations to leave.

I clearly remember listening to the news one afternoon in 1994 after returning from school: I was terrified to hear that people were fighting in the neighbouring province of Goma, North Kivu. In 1995, news spread about tribal conflicts in different places of North Kivu and some parts of South Kivu. Men from different villages would gather under the mango trees in Lusenda and talk for hours about what was happening, what it meant for their families and what they should do.

Grownups in my village also talked about how Rwanda was planning to invade DR Congo to pursue Hutus who had fled the 1994 Rwandan genocide. The Hutus were living in refugee camps in my home province, South Kivu. All these discussions confused me and I could not understand why Rwanda and different tribes would fight against each other. My Sunday school teacher connected these events to the scriptures in the book of Revelation: "Nations will stand against nations and all sorts of wickedness will happen," he said. This made some sense, but as a child I did not know why it had to happen to me. Did I do something wrong to deserve this?

Frustrated with the failure of grownups to give a clear explanation, I ran to my grandparents to get their perspective on what was happening. In a soft voice my Grandfather asked, "Are you sure you want to know?" After an affirmative nod, my Grandfather went back in time to explain many things to me — that DR Congo is huge, the second largest country on the African continent and it is full of natural resources that many around the world envy. Because of this, King Leopold II of Belgium made DR Congo his possession. In 1878, Leopold II commissioned Henry Morton Stanley (of the famous quote, "Dr. Livingstone, I presume?") to go to DR Congo under the umbrella of the International African Society, a theoretical philanthropic organization. However, Leopold II was never interested in philanthropy but instead, planned on stealing ivory, copper and rubber. On behalf of Leopold II, Stanley deceived local Congolese chiefs into signing over 400 treaties over a five year period, handing over their land rights. The chiefs did not understand the present and future impact these agreements would have on the Congolese people.

My Grandfather described the hideous crimes that Leopold's rubber traders committed against my ancestors. Henry Morton Stanley was alleged to have slaughtered more Africans than any other explorer. They would raid villages, taking women and children captive as an incentive for the men to bring back even greater supplies of rubber from the forest. Those who did not return with their required quota had their hands chopped off. As I cried in anger and sadness over my people's history, I dreamed of the day I would study in university, become a lawyer and defend my country.

My Grandfather also explained the deep impact that the Berlin conference of 1884 had on DR Congo and Africa as a whole. At this conference, many European countries sat at the table to divide the African continent into countries. Shockingly, no native African was present. Using a Bembe hunting analogy, he said, "M'nga wobe tasangwa ùbabaka kyokù, ùhebwa m'éla" literally meaning, "What do you expect when none of your family is present when an elephant is slaughtered? You will get the tail — in other words, nothing." At the conference, Leopold II, aware of a German desire to offset French and British colonial interests, managed to convince the famous Iron Chancellor Otto von Bismarck to declare DR Congo a free trade area and that is how it was seized as the personal fiefdom of Leopold II.

It was not until the 1950s that the charismatic revolutionary Patrice Lumumba led the independence movement to regain control of DR Congo from the colonizers. After years of struggle, Lumumba finally led DR Congo into independence in 1960. However, with the support of Belgium and the international community, Lumumba was assassinated only a few months later and Mobutu Sese Seko — supported by these same countries — took power. These events continued the legacy of horrific experiences that caused the death of millions of innocent Congolese.

My Grandfather told us that the Banyarwanda (who now call themselves Banyamulenge) came to DR Congo in the 1950s and more migrated to the Kivu region from Rwanda to escape ethnic fighting that started in 1959. The Banyarwanda who were pastoralists settled up in the hills of Fizi and Uvira in search of green pasture for their cattle. Although the Banyarwanda did not marry with any existing local tribes, they lived in peace with these communities including the Babembe for many years, until the fight for land and other political reasons came in the early 1990s.

Tears of sorrow and fear engulfed me as I left my Grandpa's house that evening. I went home and started packing to prepare for war, not understanding the terror to come. Although I did not know what to pack as a child, I was sure I needed to build something to carry my chickens. The next day after school, I ran to the bush to get some bamboo and rope to build a small house that I could use to transport my chickens during the war.

In early 1996 it became clear that violence was coming our way. We heard about the Banyarwanda joining forces with other Tutsis in Rwanda and elsewhere to invade DR

Congo and form the Hima Empire. Months later, we heard that the Banyarwanda had killed a Bashi-m'nyaka Bembe chief, Henry, in the mountains about two hundred kilometres from my village. This was followed by retaliations and killings by both Banyarwanda and Bembe. Both groups killed many innocent people. The Babembe said they were claiming their land that had long been occupied by the Banyarwanda. The Banyarwanda claimed the land was theirs since they had been squatting on it for years.

As the days passed, our village received more news of the escalating conflict and merciless killings. I was so confused and thought to myself, "Why can't these grownups sit down and resolve their issues peacefully?" The conflict between the Banyarwanda, Babembe and other groups appeared tribal, however political forces from international companies and countries contributed significantly. The older I got, the better I understood the political and social injustices that many Congolese had experienced year after year.

The rumours became reality when we heard of decapitations twenty kilometres from my village. In September 1996, schools closed out of trepidation that violence could erupt at any time. People started to sleep in the bush out of dread of enemy attacks during the night. Only a few brave villagers would dare go to their farms for food and firewood. Life was also constrained for the children who used to roam freely in the mountains, playing and picking fruit; outings were stopped for safety and security reasons.

Pressure increased for young people to establish the

Mai-Mai forces (local people who came together to defend the land). A couple of weeks later, the Mai-Mai began to recruit young people to fight the Banyarwanda and other external forces. Young and old were proud to join this group to defend women, children and the elderly. As the only boy, my parents were petrified for my well-being and did not want me to join. I was now fifteen years old. I felt ashamed since everyone else my age had joined and it was a sign of weakness to refuse. A few days later, my parents decided to send my two younger sisters (Furaha and Mapenzi) and me to study sixty kilometres away in Abeka, convinced it would be safer. My elder sister Ne'ema went to live with my aunt Mwashamba in Uvira, and Eca and Zawadi remained in Lusenda with my parents.

The new village, Abeka, was close to my maternal Grandpa's home and appeared peaceful. While there, I learned even more about my country and tribe. I made new friends and resumed my regular routines — from school to fishing, choir practice to soccer and thereby, life carried on in a semi-normal way. Everybody believed that our military and President Sese Seko would protect us, but we were proven wrong.

# 4

# THE DAY THAT CHANGED MY LIFE

Bright sunlight streamed through my bedroom window on October 25, 1996, waking me gently with its warmth. We had been living in Abeka for two months now. It was early morning and I followed my usual ritual of heading to Lake Tanganyika with some friends to bathe. Students would commonly tease each other if one looked unkempt so I jumped into the cool waters to freshen up, not wanting to be teased. As I floated like a starfish in the glassy waters, war seemed like a distant, implausible reality. I thought of my parents and friends I had left in Lusenda and my heart ached in their absence, hoping we would be reunited in a few weeks. Little did I know that we would remain separated much longer.

After our quick swim, we headed off to school, enjoying

an avocado and two bananas during the five minute walk. I had packed a few extra bananas and a bit of rice for lunch, my usual fare. The school had an iron-sheet roof and the floor was composed of dirt. Students would take turns bringing water from the lake to splash on the floor to keep the dust at bay. A handmade blackboard covered the majority of the front wall and the remaining walls were made up of red clay bricks. Benches lined the room for fifty of us to sit on as we attentively listened to our teacher. Our knees served as desks; although awkward and tiresome, we quickly adapted since we were eager to learn.

Even now I can remember my history teacher's voice that Friday morning of October 25, 1996, telling us the compelling story of Jeanne d'Arc (Joan of Arc). My teacher explained that Jeanne d'Arc was a seventeen-year-old village girl who played a pivotal role in freeing France from English oppression through the French Revolution. That day, I was inspired and energized by the history lesson: I, Msenwa, a fifteen-year-old Congolese boy, can be a history maker too!

In the next class, I enjoyed learning about our national geography. I was fascinated to hear the teacher say that Lake Tanganyika, by volume, is estimated to be the second largest freshwater lake in the world and that DR Congo borders on most of it, followed by Tanzania, then Burundi and Zambia. I asked the teacher, "Can I take my parents' canoe across Lake Tanganyika to Zambia and out to the Atlantic Ocean?" "Yes but we could lose you in the canoe because the lake is very unpredictable," my teacher replied, explaining that colossal storms could arise and threaten everything in its path. I cried as the fate of two relatives came to mind. Their fishing boat was hit by such a storm on Lake Tanganyika and after searching for two months, their bodies were recovered in Tanzania. Yet, this lake was everything to us — it gave us fresh water to drink, fish to eat, a natural swimming pool and a sense of awe and splendour.

Lake Tanganyika, I miss you!

During school break, my friends and I playfully chased each other in a game of soccer, made jokes in Ebembe and climbed mango trees in search of succulent fruit to supplement our sparse lunch. At the sound of the whistle, we scrambled down our mango trees and ran back to class only to have the lesson abruptly halted by the sound of gunshots. The school authorities did not think it was anything serious, until it was too late. Before we knew it, the person sent out to scrutinize the situation had been shot to death.

Fear gripped us. Many of us started to cry in bewilderment. Within a short period of time, parents began streaming into the school to pick up their children. The situation became fatally violent within a short period of time; over five people were killed close to the school and another eight in the nearby mountains. Everything happened so quickly. It felt like the sky was falling down on us.

My sisters and I had no parent to pick us up, since they were sixty kilometres away. My six and eight-year-old sisters looked up at me, seeking reassurance. Sensing their terror and anxiety, I drew both of them into a big hug as I recalled a Sunday school teacher's words, "Horrific and traumatic events happen to good people." I struggled to stay calm as anger surged within. I did not understand why my sisters and I had to witness such horrific events, especially without our parents to comfort and protect us.

Forced to become a father figure to my two younger sisters, I had to make quick decisions to ensure our safety. In less than an hour, the school was eerily quiet. Students had left with their parents and teachers had gone to look for their own families. Nobody remained to take charge of us. We shed tears of helplessness and hopelessness. After a few minutes of crying and a silent prayer, I felt an inner command urging us to leave. "We must go home," I told my sisters as we began the sixty-kilometre journey.

October 25, 1996 is a day I will never forget. Our peaceful environment turned into a war zone with shooting, bloodshed and dead bodies everywhere. My sisters and I were traumatized in the face of death, wading through blood and corpses and hearing screams of terror. We were no longer naïve to the atrocities of war. As the sun went down, we began to cry out of fear, hunger and exhaustion. We were about halfway home and like hundreds of children, separated from our parents.

# 5

# SHADOW OF DEATH

On that full moonlit night of October 25, 1996, we hid in the bush but could not sleep due to pervasive thoughts of bloodshed and murder, which minimized any fear of deadly snakes or dangerous animals. I was encouraged when we met other lost children in the bush, providing comfort and strength in numbers. We took solace in conversation and kept each other warm since we had no blankets. That night was unbearably long.

I became a father figure, counsellor and leader, at fifteen years of age. We shared the journey with two other children who had witnessed the murder of their parents. As we walked to Lusenda that early morning of October 26, 1996, we witnessed another two people being murdered right before our eyes. We were horrified and traumatized, knowing that death could call our name any moment.

"It is a miracle you are still with us."

No one would dare walk on the main roads. We had to create our own path through the heavy bush and forest, attentive to any movement that could indicate impending danger. I never imagined gunfire and stepping over corpses could become a typical experience early in my life. My belief in fairness and justice was shattered by the brokenness of mankind, greed and the pursuit of power.

War, I hate you!

To my dismay, when we arrived back home, our parents were not there. I became very angry, feeling deserted. On top of that, my chickens were missing! As a teenager, I could not understand why my parents would run for their lives, leaving us behind. Neither did I understand why war would choose to cause unbearable distress on us, including my innocent chickens. At the back of my mind, I kept on thinking: chickens do not harm anyone. Why should they be affected by greedy men? I needed an explanation, but there was none. I felt disconnected from my parents, village, nature and everything that I treasured and defined me.

I ran outside my family home, overwhelmed with inexpressible emotions. I was traumatized by the loss of my parents and by witnessing merciless killing of innocent people. As a teenager, I needed to feel safe and secure, but the only thing I could see and smell was innocent blood and dead bodies. My village was no longer familiar. Even my atùcù tree, previously used for swinging innocently as a child, was thick in blood and had been destroyed by gunfire damage to every limb. Frustration and hopelessness swept over me. My whole body felt numb and my mind went blank as I fell to the ground, lifeless. My two young sisters were mortified, thinking I was dead.

When I regained consciousness, my sisters clasped their small hands in mine while leaning on me as we slowly made our way to an orange tree on my parents' property. As we sat on the grass, my sisters started asking many questions: do you think our parents and other sisters were killed? Do you think we will ever see them again? Do you think God will protect all of us? Do you think it is fair they left without us? Do you think they love us enough to risk returning for us? I had no answers. Despite growing up in a Christian home, we were confused by God's apparent absence in the midst of war. Nonetheless, we sang some of our favourite songs and feebly prayed. We felt encouraged after hours spent crying and pondering numerous, unanswered questions about the nature of mankind, our parents and God.

While under the orange tree, we heard more deafening gunshots. It sounded like the sky was once again falling on us. Before we could move, we saw armed people running in both directions. "Run! We are under attack!" one fellow shouted. We could not tell where the attackers were coming from. I froze in panic. I looked around and no one was there to decide for me. I grabbed my sisters and we ran into the bush again.

Unable to predict ominous adversity, I decided we should run towards the school in Abeka, uncertain if that was the right decision. Our journey back to Abeka was chaotic as assaults continued. Everyone else was headed in the opposite direction. We stepped over lifeless bodies, both civilian and armed. We met many lost Hutu children from Rwanda. Only one could speak any of the languages we knew (Ebembe, Swahili and French) but we camped with many and each shared the fruit we picked in the jungle. The one who could speak our language shared how Rwandan forces had attacked the camp where they had been living since the Rwandan genocide in 1994. They had witnessed the ruthless butchery of loved ones. We listened to horrific stories for hours, crying together and comforting each other. We continued our journey with the lost Hutu children.

We came across one dead body that still held a gun in his hands. Part of me commanded, "Take the gun! Protect your sisters and yourself." Another part gently urged, "Leave the gun. You do not even know how to use it and it is too heavy to carry." I picked up the gun; it was loaded and indeed heavy. As I was battling thoughts within, my sister whispered, "We do not need a gun to protect us. God's angels are watching over us." I immediately dropped the gun.

Two minutes later, we encountered five Hutu women and their children in the bush. Only one of them could speak some Swahili. We gratefully accepted the avocados they generously shared with us. Our hungry bellies rejoiced as we devoured every bit of its soft, green flesh. We camped together under the same tree for one night. One woman, in limited Swahili, articulated events around the brutal bloodbath perpetrated by the Rwandan army in the Ruvunge camp, where they had lived for two years.

As we approached Lúùkye village, about a four-hour

walk from the school, someone emerged from the bush and warned us, "Be watchful as you trek. The Rwandan army just lost many soldiers in an attack by the Mai-Mai [local people who had united to defend our land]. It only happened a few hours ago and they are taking their anger out on innocent civilians of any age." I stood still, undecided in what to do. We knew that we could be targeted at any point, but going forward or back meant the same. No place was safe for us. Courageously, we continued our journey onward.

Many emotions were elicited as we passed Nundu Deaconess Hospital where I was born. I wondered why I was born — was I born to die in the war? My soul cried out as the Psalmist: "Oh LORD, how many are my foes! Many are rising against me." I knew there was a great purpose as to why I came into this world and why I had already survived malaria and cholera and the crocodile, but I could not see past the horrors of the last few days.

Arriving at Lúùkye, the stench of blood and decaying bodies was overwhelming. Three others were walking alongside us. From nowhere, we heard a gun blast. The one next to me fell to the ground, dead. In a split second we were running for our lives. As I write this book, flashbacks of this and other close encounters with death bombard my thoughts. I cannot help but stop for a few minutes to weep with intense grief.

"It is a miracle you are still with us."

We darted into the bush, heading to Mboko, a nearby village. As we ran, we hurdled over numerous dead men, women and children; death was inescapable. After thirty minutes of running, I realized I had lost my sandals because my feet were raw and painful. I halted, only to discover that my feet were bleeding from the many thorns and bushes I had treaded on. I was in desperate pain but knew it was unsafe to stop. We stealthily trekked through palm, coffee, cassava and banana farms in hopes of reaching a safe destination.

Intense hunger made begging for food a necessity for survival. The two days in the bush from Lusenda to Abeka were stressful and traumatizing, resulting in a faltering hope of survival, further shaken by the uncertainty of whether my parents and other relatives were even alive. We finally arrived at our school, but no one was there. I instructed my sisters to stay in the bush while I surveyed the area.

Behind the school, I saw two women and five young girls about twelve to fifteen years of age. They were alive but in appalling condition and emotionally distraught. I approached one of them who hesitantly disclosed, "We were all raped at gunpoint by over thirty men who only spoke a Rwandan language. You have to run now since they might return." I panicked and sensed my heart fail from trepidation. I wanted to help but did not know how; I could not defend them from a group of ruthless men.

I was enraged at myself for failing to respond, based on childhood lessons about extending compassion and kindness to those in need. While I was wrestling with these thoughts, more blasts sounded nearby, forcing a speedy return to my sisters' hiding place. They were safe but I realized yet another familiar place had turned into a death trap. I could not keep my sisters in such a precarious place, where evil men were roaming the roads intent on demoralizing and raping. We decided to leave Abeka in search of another refuge.

We emerged from the bush in Abeka, only to find hundreds of Banyarwanda and Rwandan Tutsi soldiers marching everywhere. We walked in their midst heading to the village of Makobola. The streets were brimming with blood and corpses. Death was still imminently near. As we were on foot among the Rwandan soldiers, a man approached us. He spoke to us in a hushed voice, as if he were sharing a long-held secret, "The Rwandan forces are targeting innocent Babembe and Hutu people since the Mai-Mai defeated them in Pemba." He continued, explaining that the killers wanted to show surrounding villagers the consequences of any resistance. There were no limits to their revenge — they would kill priests and males of any age, rape girls and women, rip the unborn from the womb, torture, maim and dismember individuals and many more evil acts. Being Babembe children, I realized we were their prime targets. Dreading the thought of returning to the bush, we continued our journey to an unknown destination along the road.

As we stumbled through the dead bodies at Ase'éci, one of the Rwandan soldiers stopped us. He spoke to us in Ebembe, one of the strategies they used to find out if someone is from the Bembe tribe. We had been forewarned about this trick so we stared at him dumbfounded, as if we could not speak the language. He stared at us intently for several long moments before yelling, "You are lucky you are not Babembe. Get out of my sight and do not look back!"

I thought I would meet my Creator that day. My sisters and I ran as far as our little legs could carry us, expecting to be shot in the back. We shook our heads in disbelief. Providentially, we survived this encounter. We were once again overjoyed to experience God's protection in such a tangible way as I connected with the words of the Psalmist, "But you, O LORD, are a shield about me."

"It is a miracle you are still with us."

I had become an expert beggar out of necessity. In the village of Makobola, we found our way into unlocked churches and created mattresses out of banana leaves. I often took my sisters begging for food, since the meagre fruit in the bush could not sustain us. We hoped the soldiers would not kill us, since they considered us outcasts.

After one month of begging to survive on the streets in Makobola, an uncle came from Ngovi looking for family. Tears of joy overwhelmed us as we saw the first familiar face in what seemed like decades. We went with him, feeling happy and secure. He told us he had not seen his wife and children since an attack on their village two weeks ago. We joined our hands to pray for them and our parents' safety. Our uncle took care of us like his own children and we relished every moment with him.

Two weeks later, our beloved uncle's life was snuffed out one fateful day. Our uncle was a kind, caring person who had been trained to provide first aid to the wounded and sick; he didn't deserve to die! He had only taken a few steps out the door when I heard gunfire and saw him drop to the ground. I ran to see if he was still breathing. Within seconds, voices were shouting, "Shoot them all!" I quickly ran into the house, grabbed my sisters and fled through the back door.

"It is a miracle you are still with us."

Although my sisters and I had seen many murders, we had never witnessed the killing of a family member. Our uncle's murder was such a shock. I cried in anguish to God, "Are you still with us?" Running through the bush again, we were tormented and in despair. Life appeared meaningless and unpredictable but in the midst of all this turmoil, a still small voice reassured me, "I am your refuge and strength. I am always with you!" After five days of retreat in the bush, we emerged again in Makobola, still with no news of our parents or siblings.

# 6

# HOPE LOST

Passing through the checkpoint in Makobola, I realized it was providential I had lost my shoes. The soldiers were targeting anyone wearing sandals or open-toed shoes, believing such individuals were of lower intelligence. The soldiers were ruthless, gunning down anyone they did not like or anyone who didn't bow before them in homage. Most of the soldiers were from Rwanda or their Banyarwanda allies and they created their own rule of law. They had no mercy on people, especially the Babembe, who were seen as a major obstacle to their occupation of Fizi and eastern Congo in general. Those who rebelled against their authority were shot at the top of a nearby hill and thrown into the river.

Having successfully passed the checkpoint, we decided to occupy a house that appeared abandoned. The owners must have fled for their lives. There was no running water, leftover food or furniture, but the first week in this house provided a desperately needed safe haven. The house was close to a big banana farm which provided ample bananas to eat. Sleep was peaceful and came quickly as we lay on our banana-leaf beds and covered ourselves with the same large foliage. We felt like kings and queens after having spent countless nights in the forest.

This peace was broken one week later when I discovered three dead bodies — one in front of the door and two behind the house, slaughtered by Rwandan forces. Terrified, we hastily ran into the bush, spending several more days in hiding before finding another empty house. I continued to beg for our survival.

Today, I can clearly remember the bright sunny day in December 1996 when we learned that the ruling Rwandan forces were arresting and executing homeless children. My two sisters and I sat down and cried, lamenting over our dismal future. We did not know how to escape the nightmare. We were helpless and every day was a miracle of survival. We began to anticipate our gruesome death, by those who were supposedly in charge of maintaining peace and order.

All of a sudden my youngest sister Mapenzi saw two children running towards the bush. One shouted at me, "*Kaka* (Swahili for brother), they are coming after us!" My sisters and I ran into the bush and spent three more days sleeping under a big mango tree. We met four other children who were also in hiding, ranging in age from six to twelve.

As I write this paragraph on a cold winter day in Canada, I can still picture the youngest boy, Misa. Haltingly, through tears, he shared how his parents had been murdered right in front of him. His imploring brown eyes looked up at me and asked, "Will you be my brother? Will you protect me?" At first I could not speak.

Memories flooded back to the many times I had implored my parents for a brother, to no avail. At long last, I had the chance to have a brother, compelling me to answer resolutely, "Yes, I will be your brother. But I do not have the power to stop our suffering." In tears and agony I added, "Only God can protect us from this wickedness." Our lives had been reduced to nothing. Feelings of humiliation, rejection and hopelessness filled our psyche and yet we were determined to remain connected to each other, nature and the Creator.

As a new family unit, the seven of us joined hands and prayed for a miracle — to survive the killing of innocent children. We wondered if anyone was watching the slaughter of innocents and if judgment day would come for the evil doers? We had no answer to these questions. We only knew that we had to beg for survival and endure horrific scenes of bloodshed and death. Although it was too much for children our age to witness, we became hardened to the murderous onslaught. After days in the bush, starvation, thirst and fear of poisonous snakes forced us to return to Makobola.

As the oldest of this group of seven, although horrified by the current events, I courageously went to inspect the situation in the village, while the rest remained in hiding. We found another empty, grass-roofed house without a door. The first week in this house provided basic living accommodations, but my young sisters started having terrifying nightmares. The nightmares were so real that we could barely sleep, save for a few unsettled hours. We would then leave the house in search of food, surviving one day at a time, often falling asleep under a tree after hours of begging.

My sisters would often ask me, "Kaka (brother), do you think we will survive this agony?" I was unsure but did not want to reveal my fear and doubt. Growing up, I had been taught that men are strong, courageous and confident. In the midst of my turmoil, I reasoned, *If we are not dead yet, then we must be here for a greater purpose. God must be in control of us.* Believing this, I reassured my sisters.

As we were still mourning the loss of our uncle, my recently "adopted" young brother fell ill with malaria. I ran to the bush in search of the traditional medicine for malaria, as taught by parents and grandparents. I returned with lemons, papayas and other leaves, which I combined to make a remedy. The medicine seemed to work for the first two days, but then his condition began to deteriorate. On day five, Misa died in my arms. I cried and prayed in despair to his last breath, "You cannot leave me Misa!" I shouted helplessly, in anger and bitterness.

I could not believe he was dead. I blamed myself for failing to keep him alive. "Why me?" I lamented again, "Why do the people I love have to die prematurely?" As children, we did not know how to deal with his corpse; we simply left and sought another place of refuge. It was a painful and traumatic way to say good bye to Misa, my "adopted" brother. I had hoped to cherish and care for him the rest of my life. I struggled to reconcile the untold death, pain and suffering around me.

Sleep came no easier at the next hiding place; we continued to be tormented by nightmares. This grass-roofed dwelling was also close to a large banana farm which provided nourishment and leaves to sleep on. Although sleep was evasive, we appreciated the protection this dwelling offered, until one Sunday morning, to our dismay we discovered four dead bodies outside; one at the front door and three behind the house. In dread, my sisters and I ran in one direction and the other three children ran in the opposite. Death was literally at our doorstep.

Early in February 1997 as I was begging on the street, I heard someone call out my childhood nickname, "Le préfet!" (Prefect). Neighbours in Lusenda often called me this. From a distance, I could not distinguish the caller, but my heart began beating exuberantly, having heard a voice from my village for the first time since the war broke out. "Come," he called to me kindly.

As I approached him, I realized it was my friend's father. I did not know his name and could not ask, as it is very disrespectful in the Bembe culture to call grownups by their first or last names. He embraced me in a firm, secure hug. Then, he pulled back and stared at my dirty, tattered clothes, emaciated body and bare feet. Tears formed in his eyes, brimming over and spilling down his face. I was surprised to see a grown man cry: this was rare in my culture, but war changes people in unfathomable ways.

"I fled to Nyarugusu refugee camp in Tanzania with my

wife and the rest of the family soon after October 25," he said with sorrow clouding his countenance. "What about Lúbunga?" I interrupted, "Does he still play soccer and climb trees in Tanzania?" Although Lúbunga was not a very close friend, we had participated in various activities together — we had fished for delectable *mikeke* (my favourite type of fish from Lake Tanganyika), climbed trees, amused ourselves with monkeys and played defense on our school soccer team. Lúbunga's father fell silent. I knew something had happened and dreaded hearing the worst.

"Please, father, do not tell me he died," I pleaded in anguish. I felt I would die myself if I heard that dreaded word "dead" one more time. He barely nodded, as if still in shock, unwilling to accept that he would never again see his son on this earth. He mournfully revealed, "He had joined the Mai-Mai forces to protect our village from the Banyarwanda. He was killed in an attack in the hills near Lusenda. His body was never recovered." Before I could say a word, he continued, "Three of your soccer team-mates were also killed in our village when the war escalated."

The news hit me like a bomb. Although I had become distressingly familiar with death, I could not process the fact that four children my age had died since last seen six months ago. It felt like death was a never ending story; the only story ever told. My whole body started shaking violently and my heart pounded erratically, reacting to the grief. My knees hit the ground, followed by my hands and head. Face down on the ground, I heaved out of sorrow, but no tears flowed.

My tears had been exhausted on previous deaths — my uncle, Misa, friends I had made in the bush and the remains of strangers I had stumbled over, fleeing the terror. I felt I was in a living hell, a daily nightmare that would never end. Despite the pain and sorrow, I was fighting not to succumb to despair.

Although I was paralyzed by my friend's death, I could not cry any more. This was not the place or time to mourn overwhelming loss. For many weeks, death had been the only news I received. Faces everywhere revealed the same sad stories of loss, violence and chaos. When I received the news about my team-mates I did not wonder if I would be next: death was my shadow. I was just waiting for my turn to die. I was walking in the valley of the shadow of death and there was no way to hide from its ominous approach.

Lúbunga's father knelt beside me and embraced my huddled body, rocking me gently back and forth. My mind continued to race in shock. I slowly began to ask him more questions about other boys and girls in Lusenda. In a desperate, defeated voice he replied, "We have lost so many since the war started." After a long pause, he disclosed yet another death: "Your cousin Gayi also passed away." Although he was younger, we had spent many hours together, along with our cousin Mlongeca.

Before the war, I would spend school break visiting these two cousins in Na'éù, a village nestled in the mountains, two hours from Lusenda. Mlongeca taught us bird hunting and how to leave marks on the trees and grass in case we got lost. I fearlessly followed Mlongeca through the dense forest to reach sparkling streams, a location that would provide tasty fowl for dinner. Unlike my village where fish was the main source of meat, in Na'éù, they relied heavily on hunting. Sometimes we would catch enough birds to feed fifteen people, while other times we trudged home empty handed. On those days we knew the only food at their home would be vegetables, beans and corn flour, food that quickly became boring to our young palates.

Memories flooded my mind of the happy times together. I finally lifted my head and asked, "Was Gayi shot too?" Lúbunga's father explained that he died of dysentery after my uncle had fled with his family to the Ubwari peninsula, about six hours from Lusenda by boat. Due to poor sanitation and lack of medication, the diarrhea-related pandemic had ravaged households. Some families lost three or more children.

I was still processing the loss of my cousin, friends and playmates when we heard approaching gunshots. "I am sorry to give you such terrible news. But know this: your family is alive! I fled with my wife and children to Nyarugusu refugee camp and saw your family there. I did not have time to tell them I was coming to the Congo, but I am sure they would have sent a note for you and your sisters. I have to go now but I will tell them I met you when I return to Nyarugusu. I wish I had enough money to take you and your sisters to Tanzania, but I only have enough for my return fare. Dysentery also claimed Masoka's life in Nyarugusu Camp," he added.

My heart broke as I remembered my good friend and her

beautiful smile, jokes and melodic voice. We had studied together during our primary school years, at the Ecole Primaire Kahunga. I had warm feelings for her but was afraid to tell her so. How could Masoka die of illness? I asked myself despairingly. As children, we had survived malaria, dysentery and various other diseases. What good is a refugee camp if people die even there? Oh, Masoka, I wish I was there to say goodbye to you, I lamented.

Death, I hate you!

It was the first time I had heard about my parents since the day that changed my life, October 25, 1996. Although shocked to hear that my parents were in Tanzania, I was relieved that they were alive. I knew where Tanzania was situated from my geography lessons in school.

Before parting, Lúbunga's father specifically prayed for our protection. Although confused and overwhelmed with emotions, I also offered a prayer for his safety. We closed with "amen" and then he disappeared on his bicycle. I was crushed to see him leave, although I understood he lacked the funds to take us along.

The two hours I had spent with Lubunga's father were very emotionally draining, yet at the same time rekindled hope of seeing my parents again. I had vacillated between thoughts that death could alleviate my suffering and hope of a brighter future. My time with Lúbunga's father and the knowledge that my parents were still alive pushed me towards hope and fortified my will to live.

I returned to my sisters to share news of my visit with Lúbunga's father when someone knocked urgently at the door. I stopped mid-sentence, terrified. If it was a soldier, he would likely exterminate us in one swift array of bullets. "Hide!" I commanded my sisters, but there were few places to hide in an empty house. The two of them sprang behind the bedroom door as I approached the entrance, my heart pounding loudly. Cracking open the door ever so slightly, I was surprised to find another homeless child. His voice was imperative, "You have to leave now! Two Rwandan soldiers were killed and they are taking their anger out on anyone they see!"

Once again I found myself unable to move or think clearly. Feeling defeated, my reply sounded more like submission to the call of death than a plan of escape: "Let's stay here and pray hard that nobody comes to this house. If they do, we will die together and never have to worry about being shot or killed again." Since I was the eldest, my sisters obeyed but I questioned if that was the right thing to do. I only knew that my mind and body could no longer stand the stress of survival. Despair was setting in despite my valiant efforts.

Seconds later, we heard a bomb explode. I peeked out the window to see throngs of people fleeing in different directions. One woman with three children shouted at me, "Run, they are coming after us!" I grabbed my sisters and followed the woman's direction. After incessant running, we found ourselves in Bangwe, a nearby village.

It was evening and we had not eaten all day. I told my sisters to hide in the bush while I searched for food. Miraculously, I found food still cooking on the stove in one house.

The family must have fled in haste. Although I was sorry that the family had to leave their meal, we rejoiced over the unexpected gift of freshly cooked rice, fish and beans. We had not eaten a meal like this in months.

We decided to camp in the bush since hiding in village dwellings was too risky. After spending a few punishing nights in the forest with rain beating down on us, we returned to Makobola to hear that armed men had rounded up all the people in the village and herded them into one house and set it on fire. This was another untold mass murder. We had averted another dangerous scenario, yet everything around us remained volatile.

"It is a miracle you are still with us."

As I begged on the streets, I heard adults listening to the radio-talk about continuous beheadings, people fleeing their villages and murderous assaults day and night. Conversely, while we suffered and struggled to survive, the Rwandans and allies, who occupied the area, amassed natural resources such as coltan, cobalt, diamonds, gold and lumber. Many small business owners were attacked and forced to give up everything or be killed. The lucky ones survived after surrendering, but many were still killed.

I wondered if shedding innocent blood was the only way to become rich. Our desire to live a normal life was crushed every day; we longed to see a day when people could live in peace. We looked forward to the day when children would again laugh and play, people would fish and farm in safety, schools would be operational and churches once again safe havens.

One night my sister Furaha had a dream that motivated us to keeping going. She dreamed of our Mother holding us and apologizing for what happened. We strongly believed in dreams since we had previously seen many of our dreams come true. Before the death of our uncle in Abeka, my sister Mapenzi dreamed about us running for our lives like sheep without a shepherd. My Mother had also dreamed many things in Lusenda, almost all of which came to pass. At age twelve, I had dreamed about a boat sinking in Lake Tanganyika; my parents had shared the story with the boat owner but he did not believe a young boy's dream. Sadly, the worst happened and more than ten people died in a dreadful storm on the lake.

With all these experiences in our minds, the three of us prayed that Mapenzi's dream would come to pass sooner than later, hoping our Mother would come to rescue us. Although reality seemed to yell "Give up! Give up!" I clung to the hope that I was born for much more than this, and that one day my childhood dreams would be fulfilled, becoming an advocate for sustainable solutions in my beloved country, instead of war and poverty.

# 7

# REUNITED

As I continued begging on the streets in filthy, tattered clothes and bare feet, I heard a female voice on a bicycle taxi shouting, "Stop! Stop!" To my surprise, it was my Mother but I was in disbelief and suspicious, distrusting everyone as a necessary means of survival. I touched her and asked if she was real. I thought my Mother was in Tanzania and despite my sister's dream two weeks ago, I struggled to believe that my Mother would one day come for us.

My Mother could not believe my reaction as she held me tightly. Tears flowed down her pained face as she whispered, "I am so very sorry. I cannot fathom how war has impacted my son." I stared at her and finally stated, "Let me see if you really are my Mother." I asked for her right hand since we have similar markings on our hands. She gave me a puzzled look, but obliged. I inspected her right hand and found the dark mark, similar to mine. I finally said, "I see you are truly my Mother." As I stood with hands at my side and devoid of emotion, my Mother asked, "Where are your sisters?"

I robotically took her to where my sisters were hiding. It was one of the most awkward experiences in my life. Unlike me, my sisters recognized my Mother immediately and within seconds were in tears. My Mother held both my sisters on her lap as she cried, apologizing for leaving them. My sisters bombarded her with questions as our Mother explained she had been searching a whole week for us.

My Mother began to explain her harrowing journey to find us. Armed men had shot at the boat on Lake Tanganyika as she neared the shore of DR Congo. It was risky traveling on the lake at that time: boats from DR Congo and Tanzania were often hijacked by armed persons on the Congo side. Her boat had miraculously evaded the bullets, but the insurgents had hijacked the boat in front of them, killing people and stealing their belongings. Once safely on shore, our Mother travelled from village to village with a picture of us, asking if anyone had seen us.

"Your other sisters and Father are doing well, although life has been very difficult for everyone since the war separated us last year. Your father had hidden nuggets of gold in his clothing during our flight but when we arrived in the camp, it was missing and we had no resources to sustain us or means to return to find you. We prayed for you day and night. We were terrified to hear about the killing of innocent people but we continued to pray that the Creator would keep you safe." She paused, looking down for several moments, "It was our responsibility to take care of you and we are very sorry that you had to endure all the suffering on your own. Words are not enough to ask for your forgiveness." Almost instantly, my one sister uttered, "I forgive you Mom. I understand it must have been hard for you to leave us behind."

Although I had learned about forgiveness in my Sunday school class and from my culture, it had never been tested to this degree. I wrestled with the whole idea and struggled with unforgiveness: they knew that leaving us behind meant we would die, or at least suffer, yet they fled all the way to Tanzania without us. If we mattered to them, at least one of them would have remained behind. After wrestling with these seemingly endless thoughts, I blurted out in anger, "Mother, it is easy for you to ask for forgiveness since you do not know what it was like to be a homeless boy!"

Immediately, I stormed out of the room, not knowing where I was headed. My Mother came crying after me but I ran as fast as I could and hid from her. I sat under a mango tree for several hours feeling bitter and revengeful. One part of me raged, they do not deserve your forgiveness, while the other gently prodded that forgiveness is a gift to self. I became increasingly bitter the more I said "no" to forgiveness. I felt burdened, unable to experience the grace and forgiveness of God since unwilling to extend it to my Mother and Father.

Sitting under that mango tree, I lamented over and over, seeking a solution to my dilemma. I could not believe it when I started crying, heavy tears streaming down my face. I thought I had become immune to emotions and tears —

I had prevented my body from responding to emotions, thinking it was a sign of weakness. For preservation, I had to be strong and alert at all times. After five hours under the mango tree, it started to get dark and I decided to go back.

Mother and sisters were still in tears, worrying about me. Surprisingly, I began to cry again. I expressed my bitterness and anger about being left to struggle as an orphan, beggar and father-figure for the past seven months. My Mother said, "I cannot imagine how painful it must have been for you. We betrayed you and gave you the role that was ours. If I was in your shoes, I would probably feel the same." Upon hearing these words, I felt peace for the first time in seven months. My mother empathically acknowledged my feelings and described how tough it had also been for her and everyone else to be separated from us. In tears she apologized to us. I did not say a word, but approached her and opened my arms to accept her loving embrace.

My Mother could not hide her shock and pain as my sisters narrated the horrors of the past seven months. None of us could close our eyes that night due to intense shooting nearby. Unlike us, my Mother had not heard shootings since October 25, 1996 and was appalled. The next day she declared her mission, "I came to take you to Nyarugusu in Tanzania where our family will be together again." My sisters were excited about the news but I did not know how to respond. I only knew I needed a safe place to live but was skeptical Nyarugusu could be that place. "This place is not safe enough. We need to leave for Uvira tomorrow to catch the boat to go to Tanzania," my Mother insisted.

The next morning we walked from Makobola to Kalundu port in Uvira, a four-hour trek, having only the ragged clothes on our back. By 1997, the Rwandan army had made it difficult for people to travel to Tanzania without special authorization, as an attempt to discourage people seeking exile there. Therefore, we had to say we were going to Kalemie, a city in the province of Katanga, situated on the other side of Lake Tanganyika, as we went through security at Kalundu port.

We boarded a large boat full of commercial crates. It was packed full of one hundred people, squeezed in like dry fish in a sack. We left Kalundu port for Kalemie around six o'clock in the evening. Although I enjoyed canoeing and fishing in Lake Tanganyika, a two-day trip on the lake was very different. I was nervous about being on the water that long. Although it was known the journey could take a turn for the worse if Lake Tanganyika became stormy, nobody on the boat had a life-saving jacket in case of ship wreck.

The journey started very smoothly but eight hours into the voyage, we had a technical problem and the motor cut out. Two hours later, as the captain was still repairing the motor, the once friendly lake became angry, threatening to capsize our boat in a furious storm. The crew finally decided to throw some crates overboard, hoping a lighter load would prevent us from capsizing.

We were terrified. The crew worked furiously to keep our boat afloat as water entered from all directions. Adults and children began to cry and pray for their lives as ten-meter-high waves played with our boat like a toy in a bathtub. We thought this would surely be the end of us. After two and a half hours of chilling rain and menacing waves, the storm passed. We all praised God for sparing our lives. The captain finished fixing the motor and we resumed our journey to Kalemie.

"It is a miracle you are still with us."

The captain announced that he could not dock in Kazimia for security reasons. The first stop would be Wimbi, a small southern village along Lake Tanganyika. We had never visited these shoreline villages before. We disembarked, grateful to be on dry land after escaping the harrowing storm but we had to face another trip on water the next morning.

The lake was so windy that it took the entire next day to reach Wimbi by boat. We were starving by the time we arrived but had no means to buy food. My Mother asked if there was a pastor in the area, since pastors were expected to welcome strangers into their homes and offer food to those in need. A tall straight-faced man standing nearby spoke up, "I am the pastor here; you are most welcome in my house." As we followed him to his little grass-roofed house, my Mother explained our situation and asked for his help to cross Lake Tanganyika to Tanzania.

We learned of a boat leaving within the hour so the pastor made arrangements with the captain, while his wife hastily cooked ugali and fish. I was thrilled to see her bring some freshly cooked mikeke — my favourite fish from Lake Tanganyika. It seemed like ages since I had eaten such a delicious meal. My Mother did not have money set aside for the next section of our trip but the pastor negotiated with the boat captain who agreed to take us without cost. The pastor prayed for us as we left his house and the only thing I could give was a brief prayer in return. The boat was small and I was fearful of being on the water again after the previous violent storm, but I had no choice. Within minutes, we were sitting on hard wooden boards that served as seats, alongside eleven other people.

I mustered the courage to ask why we left Wimbi around midnight. I was horrified by the reply, "We must travel now to avoid getting caught by the Tanzanian navy or police. If they catch us, we will all be sent to jail for months or years without a court hearing." "Jail?" I asked in shock. "Yah, Tanzanian jails, especially Bangwe, are horrible," was the unnerving reply.

It took about three hours to leave behind the Congolese fishermen and their boats. Soon, our small boat began passing Tanzanian boats and we were warned, "Upon arrival you have to get off the boat quickly and find your way. You must be careful and leave immediately to avoid being arrested. If the police catch you, it is your problem. We are not responsible for anything." The mention of police scared me to death, recalling events when police had shot and killed many. As passengers hastily disembarked, I surveyed the area suspiciously and asked the captain in a whisper, "Where are we?" He responded in kindness, "You are in Ujiji, Kigoma province, my son," while urging, "Now go, before the police find you!"

Ujiji? That name sounds familiar, I thought. My Mother

broke my pondering. "We must find out where refugees are registered," she insisted. As we hurried along the path from the lake to town, I remembered why Ujiji was familiar. This is where the medical missionary Dr. David Livingstone was buried. History class seemed like a faint memory now, but remnants of these lessons still pushed through my mind with surprising clarity.

Fortunately, we found an older lady who was heading to her farm. She gave us directions to the United Nations High Commissioner for Refugees (UNHCR) in Kigoma city. "But use the narrow path," she urged, "police will soon start patrolling the main road." We gratefully accepted her advice and headed towards Kigoma.

After two hours of walking we arrived at Maweni to experience my first culture shock. Although I spoke Swahili in DR Congo, the Tanzanian Swahili was different and I could not understand some of their words so my Mother had to interpret. At Maweni, many others were also looking to register with the UNHCR, but an hour later, their officials packed us all in a transport truck to take us to Kibirizi where their site had relocated. When we arrived in Kibirizi, the wait was unbearably long before my name was called and I did not recognize the pronunciation until someone approached me and shouted in Swahili, "Wewe mkimbizi njoo!" literally meaning "You, refugee, come!"

"I am a Congolese, not a refugee," I retorted confidently. In scorn I was told, "We only deal with refugees here, not Congolese. If you want my help you need to tell me you are a refugee, otherwise I will call the immigration police to deal with you." I could not hold back any longer, "Me, a refugee? Over my dead body!"

# 8

# IDENTITY STOLEN

Refugee.

The word implied homeless, powerless, lost and forgotten, among many other negative connotations. During my years of childhood bliss, I had never imagined becoming a refugee one day. That word signalled the end of my life — it reminded me of the Rwandan Hutu boys I had met in the bush, without hope or purpose.

I had no clue why I was suddenly being treated as an inferior person; fleeing war in my country was unavoidable. My Mother rushed over and tried to mediate by interjecting, "My son has been traumatized and may not understand what you are saying." "Traumatized, yes," I rebelled, "but I am not ready to trade my identity for a refugee card!"

I was put aside for about three hours while they finished assisting others in line. I was then asked additional questions about how I arrived in Tanzania. I was so overwhelmed and frustrated that I uttered my first curse words that day. They put a bracelet on my left wrist with the UNHCR logo to identify me as a refugee. The band seemed more like handcuffs than a source of aid. That day left an indelible mark on my life, signalling the end of my Congolese identity and the beginning of utter hopelessness.

Upon our branding as refugees, we were told we would be taken to the refugee camp within a week. Meanwhile, we were escorted to the main soccer stadium in Kigoma where they had set up tents for a great number of refugees. It seemed like three times the population of Lusenda was packed into one small area. The place was hot, smelly and poor sanitation was evident. Cholera had already started to ravage through the tight quarters and there was no privacy.

Three days later, the UNHCR announced that they would transport us to Lugufu. We were herded onto a transport truck destined for the refugee camp there. As the door closed and the smell of human sweat and sickness filled the unventilated truck, I wondered what life in Lugufu refugee camp had to offer. Little did I anticipate the impending merciless and nerve-racking journey from Lugufu to Nyarugusu and the beginning of a desperate and helpless life in the refugee camp.

On a rainy day in April 1997, we headed to Lugufu refugee camp, the second camp established by the United Nations High Commissioner for Refugees (UNHCR) in Tanzania to host the overwhelming number of Congolese forced to flee the war in DR Congo, which was soon deemed the "African World War." Our Mother explained the process, "In the refugee camp, each person is given a ration card to receive food and other basic supplies. Because this food is minimal, people try to register more than once to get extra ration cards for their families."

Since my Mother had a ration card for Nyarugusu refugee camp she did not line up for the meagre handouts in Lugufu. At that time I did not understand what she meant by ration cards because I thought people in the camp could farm the land and produce their own crops. I came to discover that "refugees have no hands," as the UNHCR logo portrays. Indeed, I would soon come to learn that the corrupt system had amputated our hands and stripped us of our identity, pride and hope for a better life.

I did not like the way many of the UNHCR employees treated us and yet there was no comprehensible protocol for people to channel their complaints. We were forced to wait in queue, without food, as UNHCR staff typically arrived hours later than scheduled, with no apology or reason for the delay. I was angry at the UNHCR agency and its mismanaged system. I wanted to advocate for the fair treatment of refugees — we were human beings too — but nobody seemed interested in listening to a fifteen year-old refugee. I started wondering if the UNHCR worked for refugees or if a select few had created the agency to benefit themselves at our expense.

By now I had also learned about the UNHCR's failure to protect civilians in the 1994 Rwandan genocide and Hutus in refugee camps in DR Congo in 1996. I recalled the terrible stories that the Hutu refugee children had shared with me while hiding together in the bush. Despite being a victim of war and now a refugee, I still expected fairness and justice. My parents and culture had taught me to treat people with dignity and to defend the oppressed. I started feeling my value as a person was being undermined by the people who were supposed to defend and protect me. *Is there hope for refugees*, I asked myself? The more I observed, the more pronounced it appeared that UNHCR staff acted in self-interest.

Another refugee sensed my frustration and said, "The UN is a corrupt institution. Save your energy, boy — you will see much wickedness committed in the name of helping us." The tall, middle-aged man explained that he was a Rwandan Hutu who had become a refugee in Tingi-Tingi, DR Congo after the 1994 genocide in Rwanda. When the Rwandan army attacked his refugee camp in 1996, he once again fled, this time to Tanzania. "This is the UN's way of initiating refugees, to ensure that people feel valueless and desperately dependent on their corrupt system," he added. "But it is unfair!" I protested. The more I saw and heard of people being mistreated, the more I questioned my understanding of common sense, fairness and justice. Still, I prided myself in my strong values and dreams for social justice and inclusion. I resolved to never surrender my dream of seeing dignity upheld for all.

Finally, someone shouted through the microphone, "Keep order." We had already spent half a day waiting in line for the ride to Lugufu refugee camp. Accompanied by Tanzanian policemen, the UNHCR officials started calling people by name. My sisters and I were at the end of the list, although our names came before "Z." The UNHCR official called me as the head of the family but demanded to know where my Mother was. "Come and join your children," he said sternly to my Mother. We were packed in the lorry like sardines in a tin. It was hard to breathe since there was only one tiny window, inhibiting the flow of fresh air. As I jockeyed for position inside, I once again mourned the loss of my identity. I was no longer a Congolese boy but a refugee, a name that bore nothing positive.

As we waited for the lorry to pile up, I had time to contemplate. I felt judged by many Tanzanians who blamed us for the war. They could not understand how a sizeable country like ours could suffer a fate similar to a smaller country like Rwanda. They also did not understand the political forces behind the war: as many as nine African countries and some Western companies had allied with the Congolese government and rebel groups to seize control of land and natural resources. I was furious to hear negative comments about my country and its refugees. I already knew my country was destabilized and I did not want anyone to remind me or speak negatively about it.

I could not stop mourning the life I left behind. I did not want to be a refugee! The Congo was all that I knew and I loved my country unconditionally, the way a child loves his first home. This brought back memories of my past peaceful existence. I struggled to accept my new identity, which seemed like a never ending curse. I needed a saviour to deliver me, but the political elites in my country and the international community had their eyes on DR Congo's resources, not refugees who were suffering.

I desperately wanted to leave Tanzania and return to the land of my ancestors — the land that held such beautiful memories, not to mention the breathtaking countryside. But this was not an option because my Mother had risked her life to find us and I could not act ungrateful or hurt her feelings. Moreover, the only news the BBC Swahili radio broadcasted from DR Congo was about the ongoing massacres, perpetrated by the Rwandan army and other militia groups. Various sources started to claim that more people had died in DR Congo than in any conflict since World War II. My only choice was to grudgingly accept my new title: *refugee.*

I still re-live the negative effects of this name whenever I cross borders or apply for visas with my travel document. "What is your citizenship?" they ask me. "I am Congolese," I state proudly as I present my Canadian travel document. Some say nothing, but others are so brazen as to declare, "You are a stateless person." Their words infuriate me but there is little I can do to challenge the UNHCR's definition of refugee. *When did all this start?* I ask myself at times. I then recall the moment in Tanzania when the UNHCR officials labelled me as a refugee and I inherited the long-lasting effects of this title.

After the last person boarded the truck, two UNHCR officials hastily handed three small biscuits to each person before slamming the door closed. The engine growled, jerking the vehicle forward. I was startled to hear some women speculate about our travel inland to Lugufu. *Inland? We are leaving Lake Tanganyika?* Though in Tanzania, I had still expected to live beside this beautiful lake that provided clean water and delicious, healthy fish. *What will life be like without the lake?*

My whole life had revolved around this lake and it gave me a sense of identity. I felt it was callous of the UNHCR to take us away from this lake, the only thing that seemed constant my entire life. Fresh tears slid down my cheeks as I began to feel the weight of yet another loss. I had lost my village, friends, family members, chickens — and now the lake. Nothing in my life had been stable since October 25, 1996.

Lugufu camp was about seventy kilometres away from Lake Tanganyika. Although this seemed a reasonable walking distance, since I had walked multiple journeys of similar length during the war, I was warned that refugees were strictly prohibited from leaving the camp or the Tanzanian police would arrest and put us in jail for at least three months before a trial.

Jail had terrified me for as long as I could remember. My history teacher had painted a horrendous picture of jail, explaining how many people had suffered and died in jail during the 1960 Congolese fight for independence. Therefore, I equated jail with pain and death. A few months after living in the camp, I became aware of many refugees who had died in jail because they had no legal recourse. I resolved not to leave the camp for fear of dying in jail. *I would rather be shot fighting for my country than die in a Tanzanian jail*, I told myself.

The journey to Lugufu was tiresome and stressful. The roads were dusty, unpaved and bumpy. Every pothole sent us several inches into the air. We would unintentionally jab the next person, landing in their lap or on their arm on the way down. Our bodies and clothes were covered with dusty red soil by the time we arrived. My Mother already knew that some of our extended family members lived in the camp. My Uncle M'mbekalo, my father's youngest brother, lived there with his family.

When we arrived, UNHCR workers were there to hand us tents, blankets, and a few utensils. We were told to line up again. *You must be kidding*, I muttered under my breath. The previous five-hour wait was still fresh in my mind. My sisters and I were tired and ravenously hungry, but we had no choice but to line up. A short time later, it was our turn to enter the big tent for an interview with a UNHCR official.

We went in and answered their questions and requested a transfer to Nyarugusu refugee camp so we could reunite with the rest of our family. "I will give you some basic things for now. Come back on Monday to start the reunification process." I asked anxiously, "How long?" She answered robotically, "It can take up to two years." Bewildered, I asked, "Why, when it is in the same country?" She did not respond to my question and simply handed us our ration card, one tent, two blankets and three cups, plates and cooking pots as well as beans, corn flour and cooking oil. She then called "next" while ordering us out of the tent.

I trudged out of the tent bewildered, not knowing where

to go and what to do. My Mother looked at the ration card to identify the plot number where we could pitch our tent. Like other families, we were given a twenty-five square meter plot, a thirty-minute walk away. While we were roaming around, my Mother saw a familiar face from DR Congo and this person helped us locate my Uncle's plot. We arrived at his plot in evening while he was draining water from his tent, in an attempt to rescue its contents from the night's torrential rainfall that had damaged his tent and many others.

My Uncle took us to Mbéléci, another extended family member whose tent was not affected by the rain. It was midnight before we finished a cold meal. We were emotionally and physically exhausted as we lay down on the rough, hard ground inside the tent. I had a hard time closing my eyes since it was my first time sleeping in a tent and the raindrops overhead sounded like a roaring lion. I woke up early in the morning more exhausted.

Straight away, I headed towards my Uncle's tent to ask what had led to Gayi's death. After two minutes of walking, I realized I was lost. All the tents looked alike. I decided to return to the tent I had slept in, but I could not distinguish it from the rest. I had learned to leave marks behind when walking in the forest, but this time there was no bush. I roamed around lost for two hours, hoping someone I knew would emerge from one of the nondescript tents. Finally, my Mother sent others to look for me. They found me standing at an intersection of two muddy paths, crying in humiliation.

At my Uncle's tent, there were no chairs. Instead, a blanket lay on top of grass piled on the mud floor for people to sit and sleep on. I sat with him for hours listening to all the factors that led to my cousin's death. My uncle lamented how difficult it was to see his eleven-year-old son die of cholera due to lack of treatment. "Your cousin contracted cholera in the Congo because we had to sleep in the bush and drink any water we could find as we hid from soldiers. He already had diarrhea and was vomiting when we crossed the lake to Tanzania. If the UNHCR had provided emergency medical services upon arrival, your cousin and many others could still be with us."

I felt anger and disbelief that my cousin Gayi had died at eleven years of age from a treatable disease. I also recounted the atrocities my sisters and I had endured in the Congo without my parents. Although culturally men were not supposed to cry, my Uncle and I cried together for several hours, mourning the loss of my cousin. War continued to inflict unspeakable pain on my entire family.

"I am so proud that you have become a responsible M'bembe man," my Uncle affirmed as he continued, "I watched you climb trees, go fishing and hunting and follow the cultural initiations. I saw you share your food and belongings with your family and compassionately offer assistance to others in need. Most of all, you stood up for your friends and family when someone treated them unjustly. We were all saddened that kaka (brother) was forced to leave you and your sisters behind. Nevertheless, I did not doubt you would be protected and your life preserved. I prayed day and night for your safety. I am glad you have grown into a young man we are all proud of. I can clearly see that the values we instilled in you have sustained you during these difficult times."

I was happy to hear my Uncle express how proud he was of me. I told him how much life without our parents in the Congo had taught me to practice the values I had learned from my culture, my parents and Sunday school. Since a child, everyone in my village had described me as a humble, polite, sociable and genuine person. My parents, relatives, friends and teachers would often ask for my unbiased, honest opinion when they wanted to verify the details of a specific event. I would tell nothing but the truth and had ample common sense. My friends at school nicknamed me "logic" for that.

I reflected once again on how much the war had shaken my core values and principles about life. After witnessing merciless killings in DR Congo, I was unsure if fairness and justice existed. My experiences during the war finally led me to the conclusion that "fairness" and "justice" are words that the elite disregard to maintain their power and enrich themselves. Still, I had decided that my destiny would not be determined by life circumstances. I resolved to confront difficult challenges with perseverance and faith, believing that things would get better even when all around I could only see darkness.

Although we had shared painful stories, that day I experienced an inner joy that I had not felt for so very long. That conversation with my Uncle marked a pivotal moment in my life. It was the first time since the war broke out that I once again felt rooted in my identity and culture. I found a renewed sense of pride in my identity as a Congolese, as a M'bembe and as a man. I had a renewed sense that I was born for greater purposes than the daily struggles I was facing. Still, I was unsure of what lay ahead, including five long and tenuous years in Nyarugusu refugee camp.

# 9

# GOING NOWHERE

Not wanting to wait two years to be reunited with family in Nyarugusu, we snuck out of Lugufu at night to avoid being arrested by the police. It had rained for several days and we felt the full effect of the downpour as we trudged through the thick mud at a snail's pace. We journeyed over seven hours with three other families to Uvinza and from there we had to go to Kasulu.

We were told that the first bus to Kasulu would be the next day so we passed the time hiding behind the train station for fear of being arrested by the police. Despite this danger, I was curious to learn about this new place. I soon struck a conversation with a local Tanzanian farmer, who told me that Uvinza was known for salt production. Little did I know that refugees in Nyarugusu were on the brink of death due to lack of sodium. When darkness fell, we crept into the station's large waiting room and slept on the cold cement floor. It was another long night. I was already sleep deprived and exhausted.

The pickup truck, which served as a bus, arrived the next morning and my Mother warned us not to speak to anyone or they would detect our accent and know we were foreigners. My Mother did the talking for us, having learned to conceal her accent since coming to Tanzania eight months ago. After hours of bumpy, muddy roads and dense forest, the driver shouted, "We are now in Kasulu, but I will take a different road to avoid the police station." He managed to reach the other side of the town without being caught by the police and barked, "Quick, get out!"

We immediately started walking and continued for an hour past Kasulu town. Fatigued, I questioned, "How much farther is it to Nyarugusu?" I was dismayed to hear it was another sixty-five kilometres and shocked because my Mother couldn't pay for bus fare. My parents had always been able to provide for our basic needs. This was yet another loss.

A Tanzanian man riding his bicycle in the opposite direction noticed our frail, emaciated state. He stopped and crossed the road to where a young girl was selling bananas and bought more than twenty for us. Even to this day, I still recall his kindness. He was like an angel to us. We gratefully accepted the life-saving bananas. After this stranger left, we continued the long walk to Nyarugusu while praising our Creator for the unexpected provision.

The sun disappeared behind the trees and we began to search for a church to spend the night, knowing it was too dangerous to keep walking. By-passers directed us to their pastor and his family who lived right beside the church. My Mother explained our situation, knowing Tanzanian churches were warned not to host refugees without special permission from the police. Before saying anything, the pastor went to seek permission from the authorities but no one was there. Despite lack of permission, he allowed us to sleep in the church since it was late evening and we faced great risk otherwise. My Mother asked the pastor for help to secure transportation to Makere the following morning, having saved her meagre cash for the last part of our trip. The pastor prayed for a solution to our transportation needs.

We slept on the hard, narrow, wooden benches in the church, too tired to mind the discomfort. Morning came and we headed to the main road to wait for a bus. The first bus passed us, already full. The second one stopped, having a few remaining seats. The pastor explained our situation to the driver. Astoundingly, the driver agreed to take us without charge. One hour later, my mother signalled for the driver to stop. The earthy smell of muddy red soil filled my nostrils as I stumbled out of the bus at Makere. "Quick, get on a taxi bike. Nyarugusu is only seven kilometres away and we cannot let the police catch us," hastened my Mother.

My heart pounded in anticipation and anxiety, unsure of the life that awaited me in Nyarugusu refugee camp. With my sisters nimbly perched on the back of one bicycle and I on another, my Mother walked the seven kilometres to Nyarugusu since her cash was gone. The path was treacherous and muddy as we trudged another eighty minutes before arriving at D1 village in Nyarugusu, where my parents were residents. I soon learned that the refugee camp was divided into three main zones, with each zone containing villages, classes and plots. These villages were mundanely classified by letters: A1 to V1, A2 to V2, A3 to V3, etc. My parent's address was D1, Class 9, Plot 4.

My heart sank as I surveyed the surroundings. Families had haphazardly arranged square tarps as long tent-like structures. A wispy tree branch was positioned horizontally to balance two vertical branches at opposite ends of each tent. A tarp was draped over the horizontal branch and formed two long sides. The remaining two short sides were hand-built with a mud and grass compound. A door-shaped rectangle was carved out of one of the short walls and served as the tent entrance. Muddy paths had been carved between the rows of tents. The tents were squeezed so closely together that a person could barely pass between them.

Families sat outside their mud-stained tents on makeshift benches, gazing nowhere. *Why are there so many people doing nothing?* I asked myself. *Why are they not cultivating crops or working?* Several girls about my age passed with sweat dripping off their faces, carrying large loads of firewood on their heads. People extended passing greetings, sparking a brief smile or short laugh.

"Le préfet!" My Father's unmistakable voice disrupted my observations. He hurried through the mud towards me. It was the first time I had seen him since September 1996, when my sisters and I had left Lusenda for Abeka. My whole body tensed and my arms seemed glued to my body. I was still traumatized by abandonment when my parents had fled, leaving us to fend for our lives, alone in war-torn DR Congo. Angry thoughts and questions raced through my mind once again.

Tears streamed down my Father's face as he audibly sobbed. I had never seen him cry before. "It was so hard to be separated from you, my son. We mourned your absence and prayed for your safety every day," he voiced in sadness. I could not hold my emotions in check any longer and I began to cry inaudibly, unable to utter words or even open my mouth.

My tears, however, were birthed from seeing the horrendous living conditions my family was subjected to. I was devastated by this alternate life: my parents had lost everything they had worked for, only sparing their lives. After finally releasing heart wrenching sobs, I let my father hug me. As I rested in his warm embrace, I recalled the countless hours we had spent farming and visiting our herds together. I wondered if we would ever cultivate our land again.

My parents arranged for me to sleep in our neighbour's tent the first night, as it was culturally unacceptable for a boy my age to sleep with his parents. There were six people sleeping in one tent that had initially housed four and was nicknamed "Les Quatre Apôtres" (in French) or "Four Apostles" (in English)." They had made their bed with four blankets over a mound of leaves placed on the hard dirt floor. My blanket was added and we squeezed ourselves into the makeshift bed.

The reality of the hardship of life in a refugee camp and its negative impact on my family began to sink in. My Father had been a wealthy nobleman by our village standards but he lost both fortune and title as a primary school Headmaster, businessman and farmer. He had been deprived of his herd, land and the revenue that it generated. My family had built and owned a four-bedroom house in Lusenda and could afford to put food on the table, every day. Now in the refugee camp, the breadwinner of our family had been stripped of all dignity and forced to rely on inadequate food rations. It was hard to come to terms with imposed poverty and homelessness.

As news of our arrival spread, family, friends and neighbours began to gather around our tent. I was surprised to see people from Lusenda and surrounding villages. Many had been unable to trace loved ones in DR Congo and peppered us with questions: "Did you see Mtendjwa, Maenda, Alúta, Bya'éne? What is happening in our country? Is it safe to return?" Their faces reflected deep anguish as I described the violent scenes I had witnessed in our beloved country — mass killing, beheadings, rape, torture, pillaging and utter destruction of homes and property.

Tanzanians had duly nicknamed Nyarugusu "Zaire ndogo" or "little Zaire" (the name late President Mobutu gave our country during his nearly thirty-year dictatorial reign). Most people thought they would only stay in Zaire ndogo for a few short months but it was over seven months since they had fled DR Congo and they were reluctantly coming to terms that their stay would be longer than anticipated. By this time, the camp was host to over one hundred thousand refugees, all from DR Congo. Many of us in the camp were extremely vulnerable and suffering post traumatic stress, having witnessed every act of violence imaginable to mankind.

My first day in Nyarugusu refugee camp brought renewed emotions, including anger about war and its brutal impact on my life. I felt depressed when I started thinking about my broken dreams and bleak future. The look of despair and desperation on the faces of those who visited me upon arrival made me feel even more hopeless. "It is peaceful here — no gunshots" they said, "but we have no schools to send our children, no clean water, no safe housing, insufficient food and muddy red soil everywhere." Their stories reflected a miserable life in subsistence mode. Unlike many in this camp, I had become immune to the sound of gunshots and thought I could live with shooting if it meant I could go back to school.

Within the first week in Nyarugusu refugee camp, I had seen more people crammed into a small site than I had ever witnessed in my entire life. I had never lived in a village with a population of twenty thousand, let alone one hundred thousand. Voices filled the air by day and the wind carried their cries by night, often keeping me awake long past midnight. Clusters of people gathered at every corner, seeking a way to pass the time.

Almost everyone in the camp was jobless except a few hired by the UNHCR as administrative helpers and general labourers. During sunny days, the heat overwhelmed our tents and smelly dust forced its way into our nostrils, however this did not prevent us from spending the majority of our time discussing politics, injustice, poverty, UN policies and its impact on our lives. It was fascinating to hear people share their values and beliefs on various topics. I enjoyed participating in these discussions.

Nyarugusu refugee camp had higher birth and mortality rates than I was aware of anywhere else; births and deaths occurred daily in the camp. As a new refugee, I felt it was absurd that people in such dire conditions would continue to have so many children, until I learned that children meant additional ration cards, a necessity for survival. Also, in the camp, we strongly believed we had lost hundreds of thousands during the war; therefore, as survivors we had a moral responsibility to reproduce more children to one day return to DR Congo to defend the land of our ancestors.

My parents explained that the only source of food was the UNHCR distribution tent. My first Friday morning in Nyarugusu found me lined up with my Mother and two sisters to receive food rations. Although my two sisters and I did not have a ration card for this camp, we accompanied my Mother to help carry the food home. That grey, rainy day matched my mood. I felt angry that my parents, who had been fully capable of providing for us in the Congo, were now reduced to paupers, forced to rely on meagre handouts from the UN.

The line inched forward at a snail's pace and I thought we would never get to the front. People were grouped according to family size. Each group had a volunteer leader who would receive the food from a middle-aged, clean-shaven Tanzanian male wearing a blue UNHCR vest. Finally, six hours later, our turn came. A few Congolese men were hired to carry the food from a big storage tent to the distribution point where packages of food and a few jars of oil were equally distributed to families. Maize (corn), dark beans, chickpeas and mung beans formed the largest portion of our diet, not because of any inherent preference for these foods, but because there wasn't any choice.

We had minimal to eat, since provisions from the UN were limited. Provisions constituted of four kilograms of corn flour, two kilograms of beans or peas, a half-litre of cooking oil, two cups of soya bean flour and a little salt to last two weeks, per person. Malnutrition was high since we had to subsist on approximately 1,000 calories daily. Only a select few, employed by the UNHCR, could supplement their diets with tea, coffee, sugar, milk and rice. My parents were unsuccessful in attaining work at that time.

Life in Nyarugusu refugee camp became unbearably difficult because my two sisters and I did not have a ration card. We survived on the portion allotted to my parents and other sisters. As a family of eight with rations for only five, our food ran out before it could be replenished. My family began to practice forced fasting: many days we would only eat once. At times, I envied my begging life in DR Congo, but I dared not do this in the camp for fear of shaming my family.

## 10

# THE DAILY GRIND

One day my Father came home excited, unable to hide his exuberance. He shared that he had met a Tanzanian farmer who wanted help and although my parents were afraid of being caught by the police, they decided to take the risk. My parents and I started going outside the camp to labour on Tanzanian farms, in exchange for freshly harvested sweet potatoes, green beans, tomatoes and sometimes fruit. Upon returning to camp, I would fetch water from taps installed in limited locations around the camp. Often I had to stand in queue for over two hours to obtain water for cooking, washing dishes and showering.

While I was astounded at all the changes in my life, in the midst of our daily struggles, a glimmer of hope appeared. My Father assembled us one evening to announce the good news: schools would open for the first time in Nyarugusu refugee camp. He also proudly declared that he had secured a position as a primary school teacher, with school starting the next day. However, I was disappointed to learn that the UNHCR did not have a "mandate" to provide high school education. I asked myself, *what is a mandate and why do they need one to teach us high school?* I asked my Father the meaning of "mandate" since we had neither Google internet nor dictionary. He explained that a mandate defined the specific issues that the UNHCR could address in the camp. I felt it was inexcusable not to provide high school education, mandate or not.

I felt the lack of a mandate was a dream killer since I valued education and saw hope for myself and the world through this lens. I felt this was the most unwise decision a worldwide respected agency could make, knowing the positive impact education could have on the lives of present and future refugees. The failure to provide for our education reminded me of the Rwandan genocide in 1994, when the UN failed to protect innocent people because their mandate did not allow it.

I mused, *if the UN cannot provide for our education — something which they know will benefit us in the long term— why do they exist, other than to make us live in a camp with no future?* We all knew through our own experiences and word of mouth that the number of premature pregnancies, rape, delinquency and other social problems among the high school population was growing at an alarming rate in the camp. As the saying goes, "An idle mind is the workshop of the devil." So true, yet we were at the mercy of an organization that had no vision for our future, other than to contain us, restricting self-determination and self-actualization.

On top of the stressful circumstances surrounding life in the camp, I would say that everyone there had gone through traumatic events and could benefit from counselling or psychotherapy. It is true that not everyone who has experienced traumatic events develops post traumatic stress disorder, but what about the ten percent or more who do? Given my own experience, I thought it was imperative that people had access to trauma-healing services. Unfortunately, the camp did not provide this type of support. I wrestled with these and many other questions about justice, corruption and the needs of my fellow refugees.

Indeed, growing up in the Bembe culture, we learned various social preparedness practices that enabled us to develop resilience, but life in Nyarugusu refugee camp made me feel disconnected from my culture and other healing measures. As children we were trained to embrace suffering and pain with courage. I knew that life on earth would never be stress-free, but it was heart-wrenching to comprehend one hundred thousand people drifting from day to day, with little hope for positive change. Nevertheless, I could still remember being told as a child to find strength in knowing that I am not the first one to experience pain: every living person has experienced pain and the Creator is there to comfort and see us through it. At least for me, these teachings became my own source of hope and courage to keep pursuing the greater purpose for which I believed I was born.

When tangible solutions to the many social problems were not forthcoming, the Babembe in the camp resorted to traditional teachings. Clans and families sought ways to address what many perceived as "UN-created problems," since many of these issues had not existed before. The interventions reminded youth of the value of community, respect and the need to develop resilience. I can still remember attending many of these meetings where elders and youth shared leadership roles.

These sessions focused on developing community resilience by identifying skills and talents that members had developed through their experiences. Songs became an integral part of these meetings where knowledge and experiences were shared. Elders and youth leaders chose songs that spoke to specific life events and how they had built resilience. These meeting places became a safe refuge for us to cry and acknowledge the pain that war had imposed on us. Until that time, I did not fully comprehend the incredible curative power that existed in our relationship with others and the Creator.

My Father's words rang true as I attended these sessions: "Human beings are restored to something more authentic and salient through suffering and pain." As more clans became engaged in the traditional meetings, many youth were energized and regained hope. Although we were still left to determine our own destinies, leaders from other refugee camps became a source of great ideas. People became convinced that education was the key to address premature pregnancies, delinquency and other social problems.

I still remember that joyous day when the elders announced that they would establish high schools. We had no lack of qualified teachers: many refugees had been high school teachers in DR Congo and volunteered to teach. The big question was where to get materials and other necessary supplies. To this the leaders boldly responded, "We will start and the rest will take care of itself."

I was so excited about going back to school because I viewed education as a transformative power, giving hope for the future. I once again started thinking about my childhood dream of becoming a lawyer. Talking with my Father one night, I asked him if he thought I could still pursue my dream. He hesitantly nodded, then explained, "We have to take things one day at a time now. We cannot predict a lot in our current situation. I do not want you to dream less but I want you to take into account the circumstances around us and be realistic. I am more than confident that you will one day finish high school and get a university degree but right now, I do not know how that will happen. However, I trust it will happen before I die." Although I knew that my Father could not afford to pay for my education, I was uplifted to hear his words of encouragement and prophecy.

I was prepared to face any kind of struggle in order to continue my studies, to be better equipped to inspire others to reach their full God-given potential. I knew one day my experiences would become a source of strength and a message of hope for others, but I did not know how this would happen. Understanding I could not control the future, I decided to live one day at a time with a focus on encouraging others. My big smile generated multiple opportunities every day. I did not hesitate to pass it on to the familiar and unfamiliar, as I met them on the paths in Nyarugusu refugee camp. I quickly learned how contagious and therapeutic it was for myself and others.

The long-awaited day arrived when several high schools opened in Nyarugusu refugee camp. I had few elective courses since I had already decided to specialize in education. In DR Congo's educational system, after completing the first two years, students must choose an area of specialization for the remaining four years of high school.

The first week of school was chaotic — no benches for students or blackboards for teachers and classes were held under a canopy of trees, but it gave me a shaky sense of potential. Everything in me was quickened: I would smile bigger, sing louder, study harder and help others more. I felt alive once again. Noting the change, my Mother commented, "I see how much you love school. I am proud of you." Every morning, I would wake up at 6 a.m. and get ready for school, walking twenty minutes from D1 to my high school in N2, methodically named after the quarters it was established in. During the first week of school, I met Andrien, Mukandama and Búbasha, fellow students who would become life-long friends. Búbasha and I became best friends and he remains closer than a brother, even today.

Our school continued to meet under trees and after several days of spreading blankets on the dusty red soil, our teacher realized that we needed benches. He instructed the boys to make benches and Búbasha and I fashioned a bench that would sit four so we could share it with the two girls we liked. The girls happily perched beside Búbasha and me because we had a very good reputation, treating others with respect, love and kindness. We were also smart, hardworking and well-behaved students. We never wavered as high achievers: Búbasha was often the top student of our class while I was either second or third. Unfortunately, our outdoor classes were often interrupted by rain, forcing us to grab our books and seek shelter in nearby tents.

Under the shade of trees, we listened to our teachers impart knowledge. Since the UNHCR did not have a "mandate" to pay our teachers, each student had to contribute two cups of beans monthly for school fees. This was problematic for my family since my two sisters and I still did not have ration cards and we were always short on food, but my parents sacrificed to allow me to go to high school. I was always grateful — and still am today — to my parents and other sisters who sacrificed their precious portion of beans to pay for my high school education.

Since Nyarugusu refugee camp was composed of people from all over Fizi, Uvira, Bukavu and other parts of DR Congo, we had highly educated teachers in the camp. Most of my high school teachers held university degrees. Many of our teachers had longstanding involvement in the Congolese educational system and knew their subjects inside and out. We had no textbooks the first year of school, but we were proud of our over-qualified teachers, who relied heavily on handwritten notes or a single textbook someone had managed to escape with during the war.

Not everyone spoke Ebembe or Swahili in the camp. It was also the first time for me to attend school with people from as far as Bukavu and Kalemie. Although our existence was miserable, I was exposed to different philosophies and ways of life. Both my primary and high school education in DR Congo were in Christian schools and although religion was a subject in the camp, the high school was not affiliated with any religion. My first year of school passed quickly and I successfully completed Form 3 (equivalent to year three of high school), despite a late start to the school year.

Life in Nyarugusu refugee camp remained burdensome for my family since efforts to obtain our ration cards proved futile. We went for interviews and followed up often, to no avail. UN staff made promises but nothing materialized. The first year came to an end with no confidence we would get the desperately needed ration cards. Since we were not able to register as refugees in the camp, we could not receive items given to registered refugees such as food, soap, second or third or fourth hand-me-down clothes, blankets and cooking utensils. In DR Congo, these items would have seemed insignificant, but within the camp, they seemed like major losses. Still, I clung to the hope that my life would one day change through education.

Christmas came quickly and I was eager to see how my family and friends would celebrate this important holiday in the camp. In DR Congo, my parents would slaughter a cow and some chickens for Christmas and New Year's celebrations. Christmas was always celebrated with hundreds of people gathered at church. In my home village, my parents were very involved in our local church and would always offer to host visitors.

I was fascinated to see how people managed to maintain the same traditions despite the hardships in Nyarugusu refugee camp. Churches encouraged their members to give beans and corn flour from the little they had. I was surprised to receive a free meal at my first Christmas gathering in the camp: the churches had joined together to prepare food for one thousand five hundred people who had gathered to celebrate. Unlike in DR Congo, we did not have any fish or fruit, but I gratefully accepted the beans and ugali.

Most importantly, it was refreshing to see how purposeful my people were in maintaining and transmitting their culture to the younger generation. I felt proud to be part of a culture that encouraged its people to share, even when they had a small amount. Youth choirs graced us with their harmonious melodies, bringing the music of heaven to earth that day. The songs and preaching made us forget our daily struggles and encouraged us to focus on the spiritual and eternal promises that never change. People found hope and inner power by connecting with others and their Creator.

I returned home heartened from that Christmas service. It was not until midnight that it started raining and I was jolted back to the harsh reality of camp life. I thought I had become accustomed to rainy nights and leaky tents, but that night, something inside me snapped. It was too much. Heavy rain soon gave way to heavy winds, thunder and lightning. Water began flowing through our tent like a river, forcing us out of bed. We divided responsibilities in a desperate attempt to save our belongings: four men held down the corners of the tent to prevent it from blowing away, one neighbour upheld the blankets and I was given ten kilograms of corn flour to shield from the rain. This was the only food my neighbours had and I fought with all my might to keep the rain from ruining it.

Suddenly, a woman's screams pierced the darkness, "Help! Somebody help us!" Two of my neighbours ran to her rescue. The water-laden tent had collapsed on a mother and her three children. I also ran to prevent her belongings from being blown away. Despite my valiant efforts, the heavy rain found its way into the corn flour. I blamed myself for the loss, especially since it meant even more meagre rations until the next food distribution a few weeks away. Many had lost their food, tents and other belongings. *What kind of a life is this, where even the rain steals your food?* In the midst of my sadness and anger over the damage caused by the torrential rain, I was thankful to be alive another day.

After several months of relentless storms, refugees called for a meeting with UNHCR officials to ask for new tents, since the storms had left many without shelter. The meeting was held at the food distribution centre with more than two thousand people in attendance. Several UNHCR officials, well-dressed in suits and ties, attended the meeting.

Like many others, I was anxious to hear the UNHCR's response to our dilemma, so I skipped school to attend. One female UN official growled, "You monkeys are grateful for nothing. All you do is complain and complain even when you are given free food and a safe place to sleep. The meeting is over!" These words reverberated like an atomic explosion: "Over?" We had not even started the meeting!

I was heartbroken to see that our simple request for adequate shelter was callously ignored. I had observed many people in DR Congo, as well as within the camp, use their authority and education to benefit others, so I was disconcerted to see power used to crush others. On the other hand, we had witnessed corruption in other UN offices, so it was not a complete surprise that a top official would spew such words of hatred.

Still astonished and dismayed by the verbal assault hurled at us, I felt an urge to review my own life. I was reminded to treat people with respect and dignity despite their race, colour or socioeconomic status. The following day I slipped off to a quiet place in the forest, just outside the camp. There I made a covenant with myself to use my education to benefit, not debase others. I used this quiet time as an opportunity for self-talk: *I will never use my power to abuse others like that UN official*, I told myself. Again and again, I was thankful that my parents and culture had instilled values of impartiality, respect for human dignity and a strong sense of community.

I returned home that day rejuvenated, yet the pain of everyday life continued to weigh heavily on me. At such times, I recalled my Grandpa's words of wisdom and eloquent discourses against oppression, which continually encouraged me to look beyond desperate situations, seeking ways to make the world a better place. Like all Babembe children, I acquired knowledge mainly through observation and storytelling. We were meant to learn through imitation and emulation, not through questions. As it is in many Congolese traditions, questions were considered a nuisance in my household; adults imparted information as they considered necessary.

Despite the fact we were in a refugee camp, my life and that of most Babembe was shaped by customs and rituals. This was the alpha and omega of our existence as a people and it went unquestioned. As boys we followed the path laid out by our fathers; girls led the same lives as their mothers. Without being told, I soon assimilated the elaborate rules that governed the relations between men and women. As early as I could remember, I had already discovered that to neglect one's ancestors would bring ill-fortune and failure in life. If you dishonoured your ancestors, the only way to atone for your wrongdoing was to consult with a traditional healer or tribal elder, who purportedly communicated with the ancestors and conveyed profound apologies.

Despite the daily grind in Nyarugusu refugee camp, our customs and rituals and gatherings as Babembe enabled us to maintain a semblance of distinctiveness, instead of becoming lost in the myriad of nameless faces, lines and numbers assigned to identify us. We fought to survive and struggled to come up with viable solutions to lead to a brighter future. I firmly believed educational advancement was paramount. Little did I know that it would be an overwhelming struggle to raise the funds to continue my education.

# 11

# EDUCATION: FOR WHAT?

Soon, our school fees were raised to one hundred Tanzanian shillings each month (about fifty cents). In our feisty determination to raise the newly imposed school fee, we began to forage for bamboo. There was a high demand for bamboo in the camp because it was used to construct more durable housing. We would wake up around 4 a.m. and traverse an entire day outside the camp in search of the elusive bamboo. We would return in the evening carrying on our heads a dozen or more bamboo sticks, each several meters long; no wonder my height was stunted. My friends and I were ravenous, thirsty and dead tired after the long day, but bamboo sales enabled me to start the next school year in September 1998, in a new facility constructed by some Norwegian churches.

A few months into the school year, students were saddened by the news that approximately one thousand Babembe were massacred in Makobola on December 30, 1998, by the Banyarwanda and allies of the Rwandan army. I could not imagine how hatred could snuff out that many lives in a village that had once been my home for several months. A monument exists to this day in memory of those slaughtered.

Thanks to Tanzanian bamboo, my dream of attending high school remained a reality. However, I worried about where I could complete the national high school exam and receive my diploma. This exam could only be administered by the Congolese Ministry of Education and covered our entire six years of high school. Without passing this exam, no one could graduate or pursue higher education, in DR Congo or abroad. For this reason, my dream of a university education seemed elusive. Many students had finished their high school courses, but still had not graduated since the mandatory exam was offered nowhere in Tanzania, only in DR Congo. Nonetheless, we prayed that the Congolese government would have mercy on us.

One day in February 2000, a delegation from the Ministry of Education as well as other government officials from DR Congo arrived in Nyarugusu refugee camp. They held a brief meeting with the high school principals and teachers. I wondered about the outcome of that meeting, but months later there was still no news. I knew time was running out because exams were held nationwide on the same date each June. I dreamed of being the first in my family to attend university. However, life in the camp made me despair of ever attaining higher education. Not knowing the government's final decision caused me to plummet into what I now know as depression.

Songs and shouts of jubilation rang out from every corner of the camp when the Nyarugusu education coordinator officially announced that President Laurent Kabila had approved that the national exams be offered to camp refugees. Overjoyed, we burst out of the schools, marching on the streets and saluting the President's decision. We saw in him a true patriot who wanted the best for his people, knowing the future was in the next generation. Only a few weeks remained to prepare for the national exams. We were under intense pressure — a certain number of us had to pass for the government to allow the exam to be administered to Nyarugusu students in future years.

Before we knew it, time came for the exam's two-day dissertation which involved writing an essay on a given topic. The government did not allow the exam to be conducted in Nyarugusu refugee camp due to lack of facilities. We were told that the exams would be in Kigoma town, one hundred and fifty kilometres from the camp. *Kigoma! I will see Lake Tanganyika,* I thought excitedly. Camp elders persistently negotiated with the UNHCR to provide the transportation and necessary food for our trip to Kigoma for all five hundred candidates. We were relieved when they agreed.

The first part of the exam went well and we returned to Nyarugusu refugee camp to prepare for the major part, a four-day review of all subjects. I was scared to death about my options for higher education if I failed, however I did not allow those feelings to control me. I did everything I could to prepare, spending countless nights with friends studying at the hospital; it was the only place that had a generator and produced light throughout the night.

The night before the final exam, my Grandpa Msenwa and family had spent hours praying for me. I was happy when Grandpa had arrived in Nyarugusu refugee camp in 1999 since I loved to listen to his eloquent storytelling. Even though I had not completed the four-day exam, a family member had dreamed and another prophesied about my success. I strongly believed these dreams would come true, just as my family and I had seen other dreams come to pass.

We stayed at Kihinga Newman College in Kigoma where we were served hot porridge and boiled sweet potatoes for breakfast before the four arduous days of testing began. Security was tight at the exam centre and students were strictly prohibited from bringing in anything except two pens and a pencil. We were each assigned a desk with a unique number. None of my friends were in the same room.

After singing our national anthem, all eyes were fixed on the educational delegate. He ripped open the packages that would determine our educational future in front of Tanzanian police, UNHCR representatives, Congolese Consulate staff and Nyarugusu refugee camp principals. My hands shook as I wrote the first section, which covered history, geography, philosophy and civic education. I dared not look up, as police and other officials patrolled the aisles, ensuring no one cheated. I left the exam room feeling positive.

The second day we answered questions about the sciences, which included math, biology and physics — subjects I never enjoyed. Nonetheless, I was determined to face my fears and do the best I could. The third day covered French and English, courses I excelled in. I was among the first to leave the exam room. The last day covered psychology, pedagogy, general and special methodologies of teaching.

Before I knew it, all four sections of the major exam were over. I congratulated myself for completing the gruelling evaluation. We returned to Nyarugusu refugee camp, relieved yet apprehensive, knowing it would take three or more months to obtain the final results.

One September evening in 2000, my friends Alúlea and Joseph threw white corn flour on my head and shouted, "Congratulations!" Unsure of the reason for my corn flour baptism, I looked at them puzzled. Suddenly it clicked and I shouted, "You're kidding!" Laughter and Ebembe songs burst from deep within our bellies: "Washa se'éla életé ùm'tema ùle akamba," which literally means in English "if you cannot rejoice with those who are rejoicing you must be holding a grudge in your heart."

Others joined in our Ebembe celebratory songs, rejoicing in our success. Incredibly, all five of my closest friends had passed the national exam. We joked and reminisced about our high school journey and preparation long into the night. We were proud to have represented Nyarugusu refugee camp well, along with one hundred and fifty other successful candidates. Some even beat the national record for the highest grade. Younger students were very happy for our success since this guaranteed them the opportunity to write the exam in future years.

I enthusiastically woke up the next morning to plan for my future. I now held the key to university and would never let it go! I was grateful to all the people who had contributed to my primary and high school success. Yet I was also bombarded with questions and worries. Where would a high school diploma take me in the refugee camp? It allowed me to work as a primary school teacher but there were no vacant positions and even if there were, I felt primary school teaching was not for me. Still, I felt jubilant and blessed to be a history maker alongside my classmates — we were the first cohort to pass the national exam outside DR Congo and the first high school graduates in Nyarugusu refugee camp!

The elation of having a high school diploma soon passed and feelings of helplessness and anxiety set in. I was at a dead end with no option to continue my education. I did not realize school had been a driving force, motivating and instilling hope for my future. Our main objective in the camp was to pass the national exam. With that achieved, what else was there to do? Discussions with my parents further depressed me as I realized that our situation would not change any time soon.

Before I knew it, some of my high school friends were having babies. Future in the camp was bleak. My Mother was working as a security guard at one of the primary schools. She was paid nine dollars a month, but had a family of eight to feed. With much sacrifice, she gave me five dollars to start a small business. Before being laid off as a school teacher, my Father had also saved seven months' worth of salary and bought a bicycle, giving me an an entrepreneurial idea.

I decided to use the bike to purchase produce from outside the camp and sell it in Nyarugusu. Two other high school graduates started a similar business. Twice a week, we would leave the camp around 4 a.m. and ride five or more hours to purchase tomatoes, cabbages and sweet potatoes from Tanzanian farmers. We would each return with three or four large sacks of vegetables to sell in the camp. I learned new ways to expand my grocery business but the profit was very low because most refugees in the camp could not afford to buy extra food. Many had to sell their UNHCR rations in order to buy sweet potatoes or cabbage, a special treat. It was physically and emotionally tiresome, but I was determined to raise money for university.

I continued the business until my uncle Asúla told me of an opportunity to work outside the camp for a Tanzanian construction firm. With my vegetable sales, I was able to pay the five dollar fee to secure this job. A week later, ten of us packed essentials and headed to Maragarasi, where the job was located. It was arduous work, digging holes to construct bridges and doing road repairs. We earned one dollar a day for nine hours of work. Our manager did not want us to be arrested for working outside the camp without a permit, so he instructed us to sleep in the forest in Kibondo district.

We cooked and slept in a tent where mosquitoes tormented us.

The work was intense and I fell ill within the first week. I continued working since there was no other option. I could not buy medication because we had not received any pay yet. I longed to go back to the refugee camp but I did not have bus fare to return and more importantly, I did not want to be perceived as lazy. I became so unwell that my friends became worried. They rushed me to the closest health centre where they diagnosed me with malaria and a high fever. I was failing but could not afford any medication.

Auspiciously, one of my companions knew the traditional medicine for the treatment of malaria and management of high fever. He disappeared into the forest and emerged with different leaves: *m'cùbya, 'yangù, mani ma ndimu* — lemon leaves, mint leaves and another type I do not know in English. They covered me with two blankets as I inhaled the vapour from the boiling leaves. I soon fell asleep on a bed of banana leaves laid out on the hard dirt floor of our tent.

By the time I was well enough to resume work, a month had passed. We asked to be paid our wages but payment was delayed another two months. We desperately needed money to buy food to sustain us. I determined to return to the camp, exhausted, undernourished and underpaid, having worked very hard in extremely difficult conditions. A few others decided to join me.

While I was away, my Mother dreamed about my hardship and the nominal money I would earn. After deducting all the expenses, I came home with about $20 US dollars, the exact amount she had dreamed about. I was amazed by the accuracy of her dreams. I was glad to be home and had a lot to catch up on. Three of my female high school friends were pregnant and two other male friends would become fathers within a few months.

I invited a few of my closest friends to my tent to discuss dreams of university studies. We were discouraged by the lack of opportunities to advance in life: no hope for university, inadequate food rations and little chance of peace in our homeland. While working on the roads in Kibondo, I had started to ponder all possible options for my future. Everything seemed unpredictable and beyond reach. I was tired of life in Nyarugusu refugee camp and considered going back to DR Congo. When I shared this with my friends, they insisted I was crazy because our homeland continued to be a battlefield.

I was afraid too, but I did not find life in Nyarugusu refugee camp viable. I did not want to get married and start making babies prematurely like everyone else. My friends begged me to stop thinking about returning to DR Congo. After our time together, I determined that fear and discouragement would not extinguish my desire to bring peace to my beloved homeland, nor would I forfeit my intense desire to continue academic studies. I was convinced that death was a looming shadow for all humanity but that dying without a legacy was the ultimate failure.

Languishing in Nyarugusu refugee camp after completing high school felt like I was a *mort-vivant* as said in

French — a living dead man. I was afraid to tell my parents about my plan to return to DR Congo. I did not want to cause undue distress or make them think I did not love them. I already knew they would oppose the idea, especially since the news was unrelenting about robbery, rape, mutilation and death in my homeland.

Part of me wanted to leave without telling them but I did not want to go without their blessing. One evening after dinner, I broke my silence. I asked my parents and sisters to join me for a family talk. I highlighted everything each had done to support me since childhood. They looked at me quizzically, not knowing where my discourse was going. Finally, I nailed the point. "No!" my parents and sisters yelled at the same time, "We do not want you dead!"

As part of my preparation to return to DR Congo, I had been reading all available books on mediation and conflict resolution and attended regular meetings with one of my high school teachers. I already knew some techniques to bring warring factions to the table peacefully. In love, I confronted my parents with clear reasons as to why I needed to return to my much-loved homeland. I wanted to make a difference in DR Congo through cooperation and goodwill. Moreover, I pointed out the high rate of pregnancies and delinquent behaviour among high school graduates in the camp and emphasized that I did not want to be idle.

Two of my sisters conceded and my Father spoke with great emotion, "Our lives are in the Creator's hands. I think we should let him go but pray that God will keep him safe." I informed my uncles and aunts of my decision, but they

# STILL WITH US

refused to give their blessing. My Grandpa Msenwa willingly laid his wrinkled, frail hands on my head as I knelt for his blessing. Despite worries of being murdered and never attaining a university degree, I trusted in what my Grandpa said, "Adversity deepens character, develops faith and drives us to more desperately seek God."

In my final days of preparation, news announced the sinking of a boat of refugees in Lake Tanganyika. Over twenty lost their lives in an attempt to return to DR Congo. This was undesirable news for my parents, already reluctant and anxious about my decision. My Father was now afraid to let his only son go. Despite ever-present dangers, I knew I could not stay in the camp. I passionately believed I could facilitate peace in my village, district and country to some extent. I was willing to risk my life attempting to inspire my people to resolve their differences peacefully.

My trip to DR Congo through Burundi had already been cancelled twice that week because of heavy rain. The taxi bikes could not leave the camp because all paths were muddy and treacherous. My aspiration of returning to DR Congo eroded with each rainy day.

Finally, a sunny morning in early January 2001 marked the end of my life in Nyarugusu refugee camp. I did not sleep the last night there. Búbasha had slept over and we spent the whole night talking about our current situation, his dreams for a family and the perils of my decision to return to DR Congo.

Despite real danger, I was determined to go back to my native land. My Grandpa Msenwa's words rang clear in my mind and fortified my will: "The greatest barrier to a bright future is seldom a lack of ability or knowledge but more so a lack of will." My family got up around 3 a.m. to prepare for my departure. My mother cooked delicious beans and ugali which she served to me and my bicycle taxi driver. We ate the meal hurriedly and left our tent around 5:30 a.m. to join another two.

    I did not know how to get to DR Congo without being caught by Tanzanian police. I knew police were arresting scores of refugees outside the camp every day. I was still terrified of being put in jail. It somehow calmed my nerves having another two men alongside as we journeyed westward through Burundi to DR Congo. Little did I know that my decision to return to DR Congo would result in several arrests and further loss.

# 12

# DARE TO CHANGE

"Dare to change" became my inspirational motto. Despite mixed feelings about leaving my family and friends in Nyarugusu refugee camp, I longed to participate in the rebuilding of my beloved DR Congo and sought to leave a peaceful legacy for future generations. Five years in the camp could not dull my crystal clear memory of October 25, 1996 — the day that had changed my life.

I remembered my history class that day, where I had learned about Jeanne d'Arc and her impressive role in the French Revolution. Her example, coupled with my Grandpa's mentorship and my own values of peace and justice, motivated my return to DR Congo. My Grandpa Msenwa's words rang clear in my mind and fortified my will: "The greatest barrier to a bright future is seldom a lack of ability or knowledge but more so, a lack of will." I could no longer remain silent about the cruelties that were being inflicted on innocent Congolese.

We had to leave early and stay off the main paths to avoid being caught by the police. Two hours of biking brought us to the Tanzanian village of Heroshingo, still five hours from the Burundi border. In our efforts to avoid police, we soon found ourselves in dense forest surrounding the Maragarasi River. We plodded along an isolated, narrow trail that snaked its way through foliage and tall trees, intercepted from time to time by narrow streams. The songs of unseen birds could be heard and at times a flock of parrots would screech overhead.

When we arrived mid-afternoon at a small border station on the Tanzanian side, police officers stood vigilant, demanding five hundred Tanzanian shillings (Tsh) before allowing us to cross. We had to dip into our dwindling resources to pay another one hundred and fifty Tsh to take a canoe across the Maragarasi River to Burundi. Once on the Burundi side, favour was on our side because nobody was at the station to demand more money or threaten us with jail. We quickly remounted the same taxi bikes and twisted and turned through countless sugar cane plantations, arriving in Sosumo.

Unfortunately, evening was approaching and it was too late to get a bus to Bujumbura, the capital of Burundi. Fortunately, we met a Bembe man who had just finished his day of labour in a sugar cane factory. He invited us to spend the night at his house and from there, at 5 a.m. the next morning, we caught a minivan. We dressed in jeans and t-shirts, similar to most Burundians, so we would not be identified as foreigners. Six hours later, we arrived in Bujumbura.

It was a new experience to be in a big, fast-paced city. I stared in amazement at the large buildings, innumerable vehicles and people rushing here and there. I remained vigilant after being warned of high rates of theft, but someone still managed to steal one hundred Burundian Francs from my pocket. Later that day, we clambered into another vehicle heading for DR Congo. We had just enough to pay five hundred Burundian Francs (about $4 USD), required to leave Burundi.

Security looked at us suspiciously as we tried to cross the border into DR Congo. Although we could speak several tribal languages and our names and appearance were typical of Babembe, they ignored the obvious, expecting bribe money. We each showed our academic documents from Nyarugusu refugee camp, insisting life was miserable there and that we wanted to return home. No explanation seemed satisfactory.

In despair, I blurted out a few words in Ebembe. Two happened to be Babembe and they allowed us to pass security as they laughingly responded, "Mule betú bana!" literally meaning, "You are our children." We praised the Creator for opening the way since woeful stories had circulated about people being arrested and vanishing at the border. We left the interrogators only to discover that our transportation had left without us. We did not have any money left for transportation, forcing us to walk about twenty-five kilometres to Uvira.

We were overwhelmingly exhausted from the long journey on bicycle, bus and foot. When we arrived in Uvira, we spent the night in an unlocked church on hard wooden benches, since I did not know the location of extended family that still lived there. Pesky mosquitoes and fear of violence robbed us of sleep. As I lay awake, I remembered the night my Mother, two sisters and I had spent on similar wooden benches. I missed them very much but quickly blocked the wave of emotions that ensued. I was back in DR Congo and could not let emotions hinder my mission.

The next morning, we took a minivan to reach our different destinations in Fizi district: Makobola, Mboko and Lusenda. I was the last to get off the minivan since my destination, the village of Lusenda, was farthest. I hugged my two companions in farewell when they arrived at their villages, grateful for their companionship on the perilous journey.

The road to Lusenda was a mess with thick mud that fused to shoes, tires and anything that dared traverse it. At Atùngulú, the minivan's tires became firmly wedged in the muddy glue and wouldn't budge. Villagers readily jumped to our rescue. After several hours of pushing, we continued onward.

I arrived in Lusenda exhausted, hungry and covered in mud, only to discover it was no longer the village I once knew. Everyone was surprised by my unexpected arrival. My cousin Mwenembuka was living in my parents' house and Nambaci, his wife, stared at me with tears of shock. In desperation my cousin said, "Of all the violent and vile abuses that the war had inflicted upon you in 1996 and 1997, we are horrified and demoralized that you could still think of coming back. What's wrong with you?"

At the sound of their words, my body became electric with nervous energy, wanting to bolt. Perhaps they were fearful I had returned to reclaim my parents' house and would rightfully evict them? Despite their inhospitable words, I made a conscious effort to remain composed and focused on the higher purpose of my return: reconciliation and peace.

We had minimal sleep that night since my cousin and his wife talked almost non-stop about the changes in Lusenda. "Our village is no longer the same since October 25, 1996. Things have changed so much. We see death every day." They listed ten recent deaths and I personally knew half. They also narrated their valiant efforts to reclaim my parents' house from the soldiers who had occupied it for over three years. They asserted, "We did not know if there were hidden bombs in the house or backyard but we suspected everything and everyone."

In anguish they asked, "Why did you come back, cousin?" Their question pierced my laboured thoughts like a sharp knife. Given all that they had just told me, I was afraid to disclose my true motive for returning. As I sat in silence, not knowing what to say, my Grandpa's voice came to mind: "Whatever the cost, however painful the process, seeking out your purpose is the best way to keep your past and present from holding you back." I also remembered him staring me straight in the eyes while he said, "Experience is what we get when we do not get what we expect."

I knew I was a resilient person who had gained far more than experience, especially during the seven months in DR Congo as an orphan, but it still broke my heart to hear of the violence that continued to plague my village. I knew that tears would not stop the gruesome scenes in Lusenda, but I cried anyway. After many minutes, I mustered the courage to answer their question. "I came to help rebuild our country," I said delicately. My cousin's eyes widened in fear, "Did I hear you right, or is this a nightmare?" I softly repeated my statement, "I have come to help rebuild our country."

A distraught look crossed my cousin's face as he responded, "We have lost enough family members and I cannot see you join them." Within a short period of time, he recited the names of seventy-five family members who had died due to the war. The list was far too long! Still, I did not change my mind and proclaimed, "Yes, we have lost too many loved ones! This is precisely why I must seek peace for our nation. It may lead to my death but at least I am standing up for what is right."

My cousin left the house early the next morning and soon returned with his father (my father's eldest brother) and mother. They were living in Lulinda, a village next to Lusenda. My uncle called a family meeting which lasted twelve hours, from 9 a.m. to 9 p.m. This day triggered intense emotions as we walked through the graveyard and bush surrounding Lusenda. So many people had died and their bodies were left to rot in the ground.

Fatigue overwhelmed me but I hardly slept. Nightmares attacked my mind, rousing me from bewilderment to alarm over the human devastation in my once secure village. I fought to keep in touch with reality as sadness engulfed me and threatened to steal my reason for being. At that moment I longed more than ever to see my Grandpa Msenwa to regain strength from his optimistic joy that nothing and no one could crush.

I woke up the next day weary and confused. My cousin and his father proposed to pay for my transportation to return to Nyarugusu refugee camp. "You are the only boy in your family and should not get tangled up in this war. I do not want to see my brother's family disappear so quickly," my uncle insisted.

Family is very important to the Bembe. As a patriarchal system, I knew very well that I was part of my Father's legacy. I did not want to betray him or my family, but I believed that a purpose-filled life, committed to helping others, was far more important. I was compelled to stay, to expend my life in an effort to bring about reconciliation between people and their Maker. This sense of destiny had already sustained me through the hard times of war, begging on the streets and life in the refugee camp. I had to believe change was possible, no matter the odds.

I stalwartly believed it would be a sign of weakness to return to Nyarugusu refugee camp out of fear of death. Do not be afraid, I told myself, Grandpa Msenwa is praying for you day and night. I recalled his words, "In my experience as an evangelist, I have seen many people reach a point in their lives where they see no hope. It is often at this pivotal point of despair that they find the courage to make tough choices and pursue their life dreams. Do not let go of your dreams, *wane m'kyù'úlu* (my Grandson)."

The next day, I boldly announced I would not go back to Nyarugusu refugee camp. I assured my uncle and cousin that I would be cautious when interacting with opposing factions. They begrudgingly accepted my decision, while adamantly warning me not to trust anyone in our village. I was willing to make sacrifices in pursuit of peace, though I knew little of what would soon be required of me.

## 13

# RESISTANCE

While I was settling into Lusenda, President Laurent-Désiré Kabila was assassinated on January 18, 2001. This triggered further instability, not knowing who would assume power. Many Congolese wanted revenge over the loss of their loyal leader who had acted in the best interest of his citizens. Kabila was considered by many, including myself, a patriotic leader, since he wanted to see DR Congo write its own history. He wanted our country to be independent of foreign influences like Rwanda and Uganda, known for purging DR Congo of its rich, natural resources — coltan, gold, industrial diamonds, cobalt and lumber. Hence, Kabila had begun to chase Rwandan and Ugandan forces as well as their allies out of DR Congo, while making allies with Zimbabwe, Angola and others to fortify his government.

I was traumatized by the news of Kabila's death since I considered him one of my heroes. Since the overthrow of Mobutu's long dictatorship in 1997, Kabila was the first leader to act on behalf of the Congolese for their general good. For example, he opened the door to higher education by extending the national high school exam to refugees in Nyarugusu refugee camp. I was angry that Kabila was assassinated to usurp power and gain control over DR Congo's rich resources.

Kabila's murder plunged DR Congo into another chaotic and violent period since various forces wanted to seize power over the country's rich resources. Not long after Kabila's death, it was declared that his son, Joseph Kabila, would become the new President. Despite this declaration at the national level, there was a power vacuum at the local level, triggering violence in villages near Lusenda. Local people joined forces to defend their land from the Banyamulenge, a Tutsi tribe originating from Rwanda. The Rwandan government continued to increase its presence in eastern Congo and they now held many strategic military and government positions. Numerous tribes in eastern Congo felt powerless, resorting to violent means to defend their land.

During this tumultuous time, five of us in Lusenda decided to start peace and reconciliation initiatives. We held several planning discussions in my parents' former house before hosting our first open event. We gained approval from the local chief in Lusenda, a Rwandan man who could not speak any local languages except French. We told him about our organization and desire to see different tribes come together. He supported our efforts but warned us of the great risk and demanded that we not associate with the Mai-Mai. We circumvented his request since we were apolitical, seeking to bring everybody together. We also decided to request support from three influential pastors in the area. They affirmed our initiative but it was evident they feared death through association with us.

We did not waver in our goals and boldly prepared for our first open meeting. Within hours, the Rwandan-dominated army had spread malicious rumours that our organization was cooperating with the Mai-Mai, local Congolese defending their land. A week later, the Mai-Mai met with us and said we were betraying them by cooperating with the Rwandan-dominated army and their allies who were exploiting our land. We negotiated diplomatically in our meeting with the Mai-Mai and they presented us with a list of conditions, including seeking their permission for every meeting and not disclosing their whereabouts to the army. We were relieved to have the support of both the army and the Mai-Mai but knew that both groups were scrutinizing our every move, ready to extinguish our efforts at any hint of betrayal.

We held our first open meeting in July 2001 at École Primaire Kahunga where my Father was previously the Headmaster. Only a handful of people showed up, their eyes darting cautiously around the room, visibly afraid. Still, we were encouraged that a few showed interest. We introduced the participants to the vision and mission of our organization called, "Organisation pour la Promotion de la Paix et Développement du Congo" (Organization for the Promotion of Peace and Development of Congo) and discussed the upcoming calendar of events. We announced our desire to work together to re-establish peace in our village and beyond through community soccer games, art, music, public seminars and workshops.

The army commander at the post in Lusenda expected a detailed report of our meeting. We delivered a hand-written report promptly the next morning. He was angry because our report did not disclose whether any Mai-Mai or their allies had attended the meeting, threatening to crush our efforts if not included in the next report. During the month of July, we collaborated with other peace-builders and held more than seven open meetings in Lusenda, Baraka, Mboko and Uvira.

Since my peace-making work did not bring any financial remuneration, I decided to start teaching grade four at École Primaire Kahunga. The school had been shredded by bullets and stripped of doors, windows, iron sheets and benches, all stolen during the war. I was frustrated by the visible devastation in my village as a result of war. However, I was content to give back to my people. Parents contributed towards the salary of teachers since the government had ceased paying them. We received only $15 US a month but I was thankful for the opportunity to inspire hope in my young students and to have enough money to cover transportation costs for our meetings.

In September 2001, we decided to organize meetings in Lutabula, the upper hills where many Banyarwanda (now known as Banyamulenge) lived. I had learned in history class and from my grandparents that the first few Banyarwanda migrated to the Kivu province in DR Congo in 1950 and were followed by many others who crossed the border to escape from Rwandan ethnic fighting in 1959.

As previously mentioned, conflicts between Banyamulenge and other local tribes had already resulted in the loss of thousands of lives since the local people felt that the Banyamulenge were taking their land forcefully. The enmity between Banyamulenge and Babembe had peaked after numerous murders and subsequent retaliations; each side wanted to extinguish the other in revenge.

Our decision to hold a meeting in Lutabula with both Babembe and Banyamulenge was a great risk since three of us on the team were Babembe, including myself. Regardless, we were determined to see different tribes come together for peace. We believed that discord was not over shortage of food or poverty, but due to a lack of political, social and economic will to provide for basic human needs.

We envisioned a Congo where its diverse inhabitants would live in harmony, connected and unified. We longed to sing the chorus that would move people from separation to connection, from discord to unity. However, we understood this harmony was threatened by greed over resources, fuelling the killing and rape of innocents.

In the meeting we talked about the pillars of peace and reconciliation, focusing mainly on forgiveness and acknowledging the losses both tribes had incurred. At the end of the day-long workshop, it was too late for us to travel to the next village yet we were terrified to sleep in this

Banyamulenge village because of their hatred, ignited by war. On the other hand, if we travelled by night we risked falling prey to wild animals.

We were given a hut to stay in overnight but could not sleep for fear of being attacked. Finally, morning broke and we were thankful to be alive. As we were leaving, the hut owner exclaimed, "You are blessed to be alive. My people wanted to kill you in the night but I stood against the idea. I did not want your blood on my hands, especially after everything your father did for me."

My eyes widened in surprise as I asked, "My Father?" "Yes," he replied, "Your father did many things for me when I was studying in Lusenda. He is the nicest M'bembe I have ever known. He was honest and loved people, regardless of their tribe or ethnic group. When the rumours of war began, people in Lusenda started plotting to kill the Banyamulenge. He saved my life." I was speechless. I knew my Father displayed compassion to everyone but I had never heard any of this before. My heart swelled with pride for my parents who had instilled strong values by example.

We left the village, walking through the dense forest of Mount Mitumba on our way back to Lusenda, after being warned not to continue our meetings. As we were approaching Na'éù, over ten Banyamulenge gunmen ambushed us. They held us captive for several hours and interrogated us, trying to extract information about the Mai-Mai. They did not accept any of our explanations and we braced ourselves for the worst.

One of the gunmen randomly shot my colleague,

Lúsambya. I felt anguish, shock and rage as my fellow peacebuilder fell to the ground dead like a listless sack of cassava root. I stared the murderous Banyamulenge in the eyes and boldly admonished, "If you only knew that inside we are all the same! Guns will not build the Congo that we desire, not now or for generations to come. You have killed my friend and your fellow human being, but I forgive you. Many of us have embraced the colonist mentality that the Congo is only for those who carry guns and inflict violence. This is a lie! We can change the course of history and create a nation where the Babembe and Banyamulenge and other tribes live together as fellow human beings. I hope the trees and everyone here will carry this message with them."

Having expressed the deepest desires of my heart, I concluded, "I guess it is my turn to die." The gunmen looked at me, expressionless. After several seconds that seemed an eternity to me, they left the scene without a word.

"It is a miracle you are still with us."

I understood that we did not have the power to straighten everything that was crooked in DR Congo but I wanted to do something to stop the injustice and crimes committed against innocent civilians. My friend Maenda and I could not move, still trembling in despair and horror at what had just occurred. We knew people were being killed for promoting peace but witnessing the senseless murder of our dear friend and fellow peace-builder brought unspeakable grief.

We decided to carry our fallen comrade back to Lusenda. We were covered in blood by the time we arrived, grappling for words as his family came running to meet us, screaming and sobbing in grief. News of Lúsambya's murder spread like wildfire throughout Lusenda and neighbouring villages. Before the burial of our friend, we overheard some Babembe planning revenge. We begged them not to do anything violent. Some Babembe considered us betrayers, but to our relief they listened to us and did not retaliate.

Two months later, we resumed our mission to facilitate peace and reconciliation in different villages. Day after day, we walked from one village to the next, gathering men and women to attend the peace and reconciliation meetings. At times I would recall past events in a dizzying whirlwind of images — hundreds of dead bodies, faces of the young girls raped behind my school, the murder of family and friends — yet these images fortified my resolve to promote peace and reconciliation among my compatriots.

By the end of 2001, we had more than fifty representatives in different villages across Fizi district. The organization was growing so fast that we had to create a governing board. I became the secretary as well as one of the workshop facilitators. We enhanced our training by taking peace-building workshops offered by various local and international organizations.

Early in January 2002, we held several meetings in Lusenda and other villages. While leading a workshop in Atúngúlú, gunmen stormed in, firing throughout the building. I plunged to the ground and narrowly escaped by crawling to the bush outside. Later, I found my way back to

Lusenda. Upon arrival in Lusenda, I learned that five people had been murdered in the three-minute shooting spree.

"It is a miracle you are still with us."

I was once again in tears, mourning the loss of innocent individuals who had died in pursuit of peace. I blamed myself for organizing meetings that resulted in their death. I wanted to die but knew my mission was not yet accomplished. At the funeral, I hurriedly spoke, choking with despair and rage. I was physically and emotionally drained after witnessing this evil. Masses of dead bodies saturated the air, rivers, vegetation and even Lake Tanganyika with an inescapable odour that screamed of the suffering of the Congolese. Every day, the horror led me one step closer to the brink of insanity.

After the funeral, malaria and delirium confined me to bed for many days. Lying in bed, dazed and shivering from a high fever, I tried to get up but collapsed to the floor. My body was weak but my mind shouted, "You must stand. Too many have already fallen! You must stand up for peace." I retreated to bed, unable to stand, but resolved to keep trying. I lost more than fifteen percent of my body weight in a short period of time. I had no medicine or medical care. My cousin expected I would die.

During those days in bed, I could do nothing but reflect on my life in DR Congo. The emotional pain I felt for my country was far greater than any physical pain. I asked myself many questions: *How is it possible that atrocious brutality is still occurring in the Congo? Was not the overturning of Mobutu's dictatorship supposed to end the torturing, mutilating and killing of defenceless people? Why are we Congolese suffering so much?* In my despair, I remembered the words of my Grandpa Msenwa: "Greed is the single root of all that is happening in the Congo. Greed for coltan, gold, diamonds, cobalt and all our precious minerals has brought us terrible misfortune."

After two weeks on my sick bed, I mustered the strength to stand. A few days after that, I regained enough strength to walk to Lake Tanganyika, drinking in its fresh, cool water while viewing its dazzling beauty.

"It is a miracle you are still with us."

I was still tormented by fear that a gunman would storm into my room or find me in a public place, yet I knew that I could not betray my mission. I was resolute to lead more seminars and that spurred me towards recovery. I was determined to see tribes, armies and political leaders embrace each other. Otherwise, there was no future, no hope for the Congo.

A few months later, we were back on the road, talking about peace and reconciliation in any village that received us. Our friend's murder was still fresh in our minds but we boldly stood for the values that would have a lasting impact on our community. We were encouraged to a great extent to meet other men and women who sought peace for our country. Many of our meetings were successful and brought Babembe, Banyamulenge and other tribes together in dialogue.

One day, as we were leading a workshop in Lweba, the Rwandan-dominated army stormed our building and arrested five of us. We were thrown in jail where we met five other Babembe. The other five were accused of plotting with the Mai-Mai. We were at the mercy of the commander in charge of the post as there was no legal recourse for a person arrested on such charges. We spent two weeks in a small, dirty cell.

A different person came each day to interrogate us — we were beaten and denied food for days as they attempted to extract information from us. Feelings of numbness enclosed me. In deep sorrow and helplessness, we meditated and prayed for release. Our fervour to bring reconciliation to our villages increased with each aggressive act towards us. Eventually we were released and we resumed our seminars immediately. We were determined to change the course of history for our country.

Two weeks after our release from jail we were ambushed, this time by Interahamwe militias. They dragged the five of us to their hidden headquarters deep within the forest. We were forced to carry heavy loads and cook for them. They threatened to kill us if we did not join their cause and we knew they could do it at any moment. I prepared myself to face death for the cause I strongly believed in, yet also shed tears as I struggled with feelings of defencelessness and fear.

We had been captive for five days when one of the men started firing at the hut we were in. In panic we ran in different directions. I spent a whole week trying to find my way out of the dense forest. After days and nights of running, I arrived in a village called M'kweci. While in M'kweci, I learned that one of my comrades had survived but never heard about the status of the rest. I prayed that they were alive and well but I have not seen them since.

"It is a miracle you are still with us."

Still terrified by recent losses and haunted by scenes I had witnessed in the last few months, I decided not to return to Lusenda. I walked another seven hours to Makobola where my sisters and I had begged on the streets like orphans. Arriving in Makobola, I met someone from Lusenda. I was both relieved and scared to see a familiar face, knowing that many neighbours were now informants for the warring factions.

I decided to trust him. We ducked into the bush and I briefly explained what had happened. He lowered his voice to a whisper, "My son, the militia who arrested you are still hunting you and your friend. You cannot stay in this area." I did not know where to go since I did not have money with me. "Please, tell my cousin that I am heading to Uvira to escape death," I told him.

Disorientated, I wove my way in and out of the bush, finally arriving in Uvira two days later. I had only been in Uvira for a few hours when I spotted one of the men who had arrested me. I ducked out of sight, my heart pounding. Uvira was not safe either!

I could no longer stay in DR Congo but had no money to pay the exit fee at the border. I anxiously waved down a truck that was heading to Bukavu through Ngomu. "Sir, I must go to Bukavu. I will do anything in exchange for transportation." He must have seen the desperation in my eyes and readily obliged. I was grateful that he would help a complete stranger. Together we loaded sacks of charcoal onto his truck and set out for Bukavu.

Two days later, we arrived in Bukavu. I had never been there before and knew no one. The driver, whose name was Gloire, invited me to stay at his place that night before continuing my search for a safe place. I shared with him what happened to me and my friends. He was shocked to hear my experiences, but nodded knowingly. "Yeah, that is the Congo we live in. I have lost five family members in the last two years and nothing is different in Bukavu — people are being killed day and night for no reason. If someone has a gun and wants you dead, you're dead."

The next morning I bid my fellow citizen goodbye, thanking him for his help and offering condolences for his losses. He touched his pocket and pulled out the equivalent of $10 US. I was only a few steps away when I saw a soldier I knew from Lusenda. I did not know if he would hurt me or help me. I was startled and petrified to run into adversaries I was trying to avoid. It felt like people were hunting me down.

I ran back to Gloire's house and asked for assistance to leave Bukavu. Gloire took me to the lot where trucks transported lumber from Bukavu to Nairobi and introduced me to someone who could take me to Nairobi. "How much money do you have to pay?" he inquired hastily. "Ten dollars," I replied. He burst out laughing, "You must be kidding, boy. You know how much people pay from here to Nairobi?" I had no clue but Gloire pleaded with him to take me.

The transport driver laid out his terms: I could cross the border unnoticed only if I rode in the cargo section. I jumped inside and the driver locked the door behind me, leaving the compartment pitch black. The next three days turned into an exhausting, thirsty and hungry journey but I was hopeful that Kenya would bring peace and an opportunity for a brighter future.

As I bounced along with the potholes in the road, on top of stacks of lumber, I recalled my childhood song and my Grandpa Msenwa's prophecy: "Going to Nairobi Kenya, Nairobi Kenya, anyone need a ride?" God had known about this migration many years ago as I swung joyfully outside my home in Lusenda. Little did I know what life would be like in Nairobi, a city of over four million.

14

# REJECTION MOUNTING

I squinted at the bright sunlight as the truck driver flung open the cargo door in July 2002. "You are now in Nairobi, Kenya," he declared flatly. "You must find your way from here. Do not trust people who want to help — the big city breeds many robbers." The driver's warning stimulated fear of violence, as in DR Congo. I saw an armed policeman on the other side of the road and became more fearful. I stood bewildered as cars whizzed past me, high rises towered over me and puzzled people ran to and fro. The throngs of people rushing past me triggered frightening memories of running for my life. Was someone pursuing me? I felt panic but my Grandpa's words cut through my fear: "Break free from your past and live out your purpose."

Hours later I was still standing in the same place, not

knowing what to do. After a feeble prayer, a strong inner voice seemed to say, "Walk south." After composing myself, I walked about thirty minutes, still not knowing where I was heading but deeply convinced it was the right direction.

Soon I came to a church compound and knocked wildly at the door. A beautiful looking Kenyan woman answered, but didn't appear too eager to help a stranger who seemed anxious and desperate. She tried to dismiss me by saying, "This is not a place for beggars." I was left speechless by her unkind words and negative, demeaning attitude. It reminded me of life as a beggar in DR Congo, something I never wanted to do. Bitterness and anger churned within.

Despite my persistence, this woman would not acknowledge me. I questioned why I had felt compelled to come this way if help was not forthcoming. Surprisingly, the pastor overheard my conversation with this lady and came to the door. I explained I was a refugee who had come to Kenya in the cargo compartment of a truck and was in dire need of assistance. He had been urged by an inner voice to help someone in need that day and realized I must be that person! Although I believed in miracles and supernatural intervention, I realized that my Grandpa's prayers were making a tangible difference in my life — I did not have to worry.

After hearing my story, the pastor offered me a place to stay for one week. Before leaving, he introduced me to the gatekeeper and instructed him to get food for me. I was overwhelmed by the pastor's generosity and thanked my Creator for the shelter and food. Although I was grateful for a short-term answer to my basic needs, experience had taught me to strive for self-sufficiency and meaningful goals. I used that week to ask myself: *Have I reached my destiny in Nairobi? Is there an ulterior reason for coming here? What is my real potential?*

On Sunday morning, the pastor introduced me to his congregation, sharing how I had come to Nairobi and specifically to their church. He gave me the chance to speak a few words but I became very emotional, tearful and speechless, missing an opportunity to thank the church for their generosity and kindness. After church, the pastor introduced me to several people and one of them, Andrew, agreed to take me to the UNHCR office to register as a refugee in Kenya, knowing it was risky and unlawful to keep an undocumented foreigner on their compound.

Security guards patrolled the gate and every inch of the grounds at the UNHCR in Nairobi. Almost one hundred people were ahead of me and I had to wait three hours before being searched and granted entrance. My Kenyan escort assured me he would return later in the day since he was not allowed to join me.

Hours passed and I saw more people of diverse nationalities and languages than I had ever seen in my entire life. I did what I could to communicate with Ethiopians, Sudanese, Somalis, Ugandans, Rwandans and Burundians. Each shared their story about how conflict had chased them from their respective countries. Of course, I also saw many Congolese. During these hours I clung tightly to the small ticket I had been given at the entrance, as I would not be served without it.

During the wait, I started looking for a familiar face and listened to the multitude of languages. I was excited when I deciphered my mother tongue, Ebembe. I quickly joined the group conversation and introduced myself, asking if other Babembe were in the city. They nodded and agreed to introduce me but just then, a woman's shrill voice called out my number.

I hurried to the appropriate desk. Without looking up, the lady asked, "Tell me your name, date of birth, country of origin and at which border you crossed into Kenya." I knew the first three answers but had no idea which border I had crossed. I had been inside a cargo compartment and did not observe our route. "Uganda," I guessed and she figured out the border name. The lady instructed me to go to the next room for a photo and then come back. Five minutes later, I was issued an appointment on October 30, 2002.

I was bewildered, expecting more than a mere piece of paper. Having lived in Nyarugusu refugee camp, I thought the UNHCR would give me a blanket, tent, some utensils and food. I left her office, thinking that someone had misunderstood the system and not realized I urgently needed help. I mustered the courage to ask if I could be supplied basic provisions but was told it was only provided in refugee camps, not the city. In shock and anger, I left empty-handed.

I was dismayed when my escort Andrew wasn't waiting for me outside the UNHCR compound. I recalled the transport driver's admonition to be careful of robbers in the big city. Darkness was fast approaching and I did not know my way back. Fortunately, a fellow M'bembe, who I had conversed with earlier, was walking by. I told him my plight and he willingly took me to his home.

The next day I was taken to Githurai 45 and introduced to other Babembe families. I was overjoyed to find Sikitoka, (who I call Uncle), an extended family member I had known since my childhood. His family graciously welcomed me into their two-bedroom apartment, despite the fact that it was already overcrowded. His three daughters (Angela, Lucy and Furaha) and two young sons slept in one room while he and his wife occupied the other. His other two sons (Jovis and Esaie) and I slept in the sitting room, shared with his eldest son Joseph, already married with a son of their own.

I slept restlessly the first few nights in Githurai 45, wondering if my escort, Andrew, had come to look for me or if the church was happy to get rid of me. I did not want to jump to any conclusions after all they had done for me. I wanted to go back to thank them for their kindness and hospitality but I could not remember where the church was located. It took me two weeks to remember the name of the place where the truck driver had dropped me off. With this name in mind, I determined to retrace my steps back to the church.

I asked one of my cousins to take me there but he resisted. It wasn't until a week later that I learned refugees were afraid to move freely around Nairobi due to the threat of arrest by police. Kenyan police would target refugees and restrain them until a bribe was paid, regardless of whether they displayed a UNHCR document confirming refugee status.

News of arrests in Kenya revived my paranoia of police. I shared my worries and frustrations with my cousins but they mocked my feelings of insecurity, causing my confidence to plummet. Circumstances beyond my control seemed to once again suffocate my dreams: how could I empower others to reach their full potential if I faced threat of arrest every time I left my house?

I soon met other Nyarugusu high school graduates in Nairobi, only to learn they could not pursue further education due to lack of finances. *If these graduates cannot get anywhere, why do I think my story will be different?* Hundreds of negative thoughts bombarded me, clouding my hope for the future. I believed my life had a purpose but I found it excruciatingly difficult to see past the circumstances. I spent hours crying and lamenting to my Creator for having forgotten me. I was tired of asking the recurring question, "Why me?"

I had an epiphany one day when I asked myself, *What can I learn through this situation?* This marked the beginning of my quest to reconcile my past and present. I recorded pages upon pages of what I was learning about myself in those desperate moments, but more importantly, ways I could use my experiences to encourage and inspire others. Months flew by as I wrote reflections in a journal. By the end of another full week dedicated to prayer and meditation, I had discovered a good deal about myself. I needed to master impatience and conquer the fear that was paralyzing me.

I defied my fear of arrest and took several bus rides, winding through the city until I located the Full Gospel Church that had graciously hosted me. It was Sunday and the service was filled with joyful worship and praise that lifted people out of their seats to dance. I knew few of the English songs but readily joined in the Swahili ones. During the testimony time, the Pastor asked me to share a few words. This time, I contained my emotions and shared my story and aspirations to go to university.

As I sat down, someone in the audience stood up and addressed the congregation proclaiming, "I will sow a seed of fifteen thousand Kenyan shillings (about $200 US) for our brother to study." After the service the generous donor shook my hand as he said, "For three weeks, I have sensed that God wanted me to give you this money, but I didn't know how to find you." I expressed my genuine gratitude as my heart leapt for joy, sensing my life was taking a turn in the right direction.

I burst into my Uncle's apartment with exuberant joy, unable to contain my excitement at the strange turn of events. He rejoiced and encouraged me to apply to Hope Africa University, since his sons Joseph and Jovis had already applied. This university, which was a ministry of the Free Methodist Church, had just opened its doors in 2000. I knew this denomination very well since most of my family had attended that denomination in DR Congo and my Grandpa was one of their well-known evangelists.

Time was running out since only two weeks remained for registration at Hope Africa University. My heart sank when I discovered the cost for one academic year was $2,500.00 US dollars. In times of peace my Father could have assisted with this fee but our family was still in Nyarugusu refugee camp with no hope of returning to DR Congo anytime soon. Despite these exorbitant fees, I listened to my cousin's encouragement and used $15 US dollars to register. I did my part and prayed for God to make a way, believing that little is much when God is in it.

The next morning, my Uncle and I discussed ways to cover the tuition fee. He informed me that Hope Africa University had a special fund for Free Methodist Church members, if their Bishop would write a letter of recommendation. This unexpected news flooded my soul with hope. It seemed like my educational dream was plausible since my Bishop in DR Congo would surely do that for me!

School started the first week of September 2002. Four of us from DR Congo were called into the finance office one at a time and I was the last to go in. The three others were informed they had received scholarships since the Bishop of DR Congo had sent their recommendation letters. I entered the finance manager's office and sat down, eager to hear the same news but instead was informed that no recommendation letter was submitted on my behalf. I sat there in disbelief as I was told the local pastor in Githurai 45 had purposely omitted my name in his communication with the Bishop.

The finance manager bemoaned, "I am sorry but there is nothing I can do for you at the moment. If you want to attend classes, you will have to pay." I grieved over another obstacle but was overjoyed when the university accepted the last of my funds to enrol in an English class, a prerequisite for admission to any program. The finance manager recommended that I ask the local pastor to send my name to the Bishop's office in DR Congo so that I too could benefit from a scholarship.

I anxiously waited for the weekend to arrive, intending to petition the local pastor. I had moved from my Uncle's home in Githurai 45 to live with my cousin Joseph, near Waithaka neighbourhood, to be closer to Hope Africa University. Joseph and his wife and child slept in the bedroom while my younger cousin Esaie and I laid our mattress on the floor in the sitting room. Despite these inconveniences, I was grateful for their love and hospitality. Another cousin was going to a high school in Waithaka, a school specifically for refugees from DR Congo, Burundi and Rwanda.

My meeting with the pastor shattered my dream of attending Hope Africa University. He gave no rationale for his refusal to recommend me to the Bishop for a scholarship, despite my Uncle pleading on my behalf. I could not understand because this pastor claimed to be a friend of my Father and knew my Grandpa Msenwa who had tirelessly worked for the Free Methodist Church in DR Congo and Tanzania. In deep frustration and despair, I turned to the pastor and confidently told him, "My Maker will provide what man has refused to give."

15

# WHO CARED?

I was in a state of constant turmoil. I knew I could be suspended from my university class any day because ninety-two percent of the amount due remained outstanding. I desperately wanted to be the first in my family to get a university degree. I had decided to study Social Work and Community Development as a means to advocate for social justice since I understood that as a refugee in Kenya, I would never have a chance to be a lawyer. Despite the looming threat of expulsion, I made studies and class attendance a priority, permitting only UNHCR appointments to interfere.

I missed class to wait in long lines before reaching the entrance to the UNHCR office. I had to wait for several more hours after I was given a number. Finally, I was called to present my appointment paper. The officer told me to return in November and motioned me to leave. "But my appointment was today!" I protested. I had spent most of my dwindling money on transportation and skipped school too.

I left the UNHCR office feeling betrayed once again by an agency that claimed to help the marginalized. That day, I formulated my opinion: most UNHCR employees — whether in Tanzania, Kenya or elsewhere — do not care. I joined the multitude of refugees who had already come to this conclusion. When I arrived home, my cousins greeted me with the question, "Did you get another appointment?" I looked up in surprise and shook my head. "Dear brother, that's their game."

I had little time to dwell on my disappointment with the UNHCR since passing the upcoming midterm exam was priority. The finance office reminded me of my outstanding financial obligation. After explaining my situation and requesting an extension, I was allowed to continue my studies and write the midterm. I did well and appeared to be the only Congolese able to learn English quickly.

November came and I missed another day of school because of my UNHCR appointment. It took two hours to arrive by bus. I was in line promptly at 8 a.m. and given a number an hour later, being advised to "wait." Around 2 p.m., my name was called. This time someone was ready to interview me. During the one-hour interview, the official asked detailed questions about why I had left my country, where my family members were and my involvement in the war. Finally, the interview ended. After the interview, the lady told me to come back in a month's time for the decision as to whether I would be approved or rejected for refugee status in Kenya.

On my way home, for no reason, I was arrested by the Kenyan police. I gave them my UNHCR paperwork but they wanted bribe money, despite my insistence that I had a meagre amount. "You must have money. Unlike our country, yours is full of gold and minerals," they persisted. I cried inside as they took my measly transportation money. "Never walk in a foreign land with empty pockets," they warned. Given my fear of jail, I felt blessed it did not turn out worse.

Since my transportation money was stolen, I had to walk two hours to and from university each day. My cousins often worried and were always relieved to see me return home safely. Everyone knew the Kenyan police harassed refugees and frequently demanded bribe money to avoid arrest.

During lunch time at school, my cousin and I would hide in the library, pretending to read while everyone else was eating their lunch. The truth was that we could not afford to buy food for the noon meal. We purposely planned to only have one meal each day and by the time we got home in the evening, we were starving and exhausted.

I went to any organization that was assisting refugees. I was registered with a Catholic organization in Eastleigh and another in Dagoretti Corner. I received one hundred Kenyan shillings a month from one place and two kilograms of beans and rice every two weeks from the other. Now that I had moved to Waithaka, I was disappointed because the ride from Waithaka to Eastleigh would cost me half of what

I would receive there. In December I was told that I could not receive any more support until my expired UNHCR document was renewed. I hurried to the UNHCR office but was told to return two weeks later, which meant I would have to go without food until then. No one seemed to care.

I was elated to pass the prerequisite English exam in December but mourned that none of my fellow Bembe classmates had passed, having spent countless hours studying together. I also began to worry about finances for the next semester as well as where I could live. Passing the course did not guarantee a scholarship. My cousin failed the exam and would have to re-take the required course at an alternate institute, so he might have to move. Uncertainty cultivated insecurity.

My insecurity was relieved when my Uncle gave me $50 US towards my educational costs and my cousin Joseph graciously decided to find an English course in the same neighbourhood so I would not have to move. During this time, my cousin and I became closer than ever before. His wife Maùwa (now deceased) was beautiful inside and out. She was very kind and an amazing cook, making food out of what seemed like nothing to feed the five of us. They were proud of my success and tried to relieve the guilt I felt for being the only one to pass the English course. It was a very emotional time for all of us because we wanted to move forward with our studies. Despite the disappointment, we found strength in talking and laughing together.

With a meagre $50 US down payment, the university accountant reluctantly allowed me to take four courses in

January 2003. By the semester break, my increasing debt had signalled alarm bells and the finance manager, Mr. Lúbunga, called me into his office. A kind yet concerned look crossed his face as he began, "Your student debt is increasing every semester. I am afraid the school will not allow you to continue unless you pay a significant amount of money."

He suggested that I obtain a recommendation from the Bishop in DR Congo, especially since none of the other three Congolese students could use their awarded scholarships since they had failed the required courses. I explained to Mr. Lúbunga, a PhD candidate at that time and a Bembe himself, that the pastor had still refused to contact the Bishop on my behalf. He was shocked and said, "Unfortunately, the school policies are getting strict. I cannot do anything until I receive that letter from the Bishop."

I was crying by the time I left his office. I did not know where else to turn for help. I was still crying when I arrived home, asking myself, *why me?* despite having resolved to never ask that question again. I quickly changed it to a philosophical question: *What do you want me to learn through this experience, my Creator?*

I felt confused but thought there must be something to learn from this rejection. I pondered the many traits I had worked on: patience, determination, resilience and optimism. I then heard a still, small voice: humility and faith. Similar to my previous quest, I devoted one week to prayer, meditation and fasting. I was already familiar with the practice of fasting but this was the first time to fast one whole week.

By the end of the week, I felt I had gained ground in coming to terms with most of the tough experiences in my life. I also recognized I was not immune to difficulties in life — my family and friends had also experienced trauma from war and many others were still stuck in Nyarugusu refugee camp. I thought I had developed the habits, attitudes and character that would see me through the inevitable hardships of life, yet I realized I still had a lot to learn, since every experience and situation is unique.

I had wanted to be like other students at Hope Africa University who could afford food, bus fare, school fees and other supplies, but I could not. I told myself that no matter what my situation, I could live to encourage and inspire others to reach their potential. I could hold my head up in honesty and confidence. I was happy to get back on track and felt that my purpose in life was stronger than my everyday challenges.

In February 2003, my meeting with the accountant proved unproductive. I had to pay up if I wanted to continue my studies. After an unsuccessful appeal to Mr. Lúbunga, the higher authority, hopelessness weighed heavy on me. As I walked the two hours home, I could hear my Grandpa's voice, "Circumstances in life do not define who you are." I decided to fast for another week.

My cousin and his wife were saddened I could not continue my studies because of lack of money. I had pleaded with the university and met with the rector to no avail. I applied the breathing and meditation techniques I had learned to calm myself down during long, solitary walks.

It was the only way I could stay sane in the midst of my turmoil. I was proud I had advocated for myself, although unsuccessfully. I felt my anxiety subside as I remembered my Father's words from many years ago, "It is through struggle that human beings are transformed into something more authentic and striking."

As I turned off the main street to head home, three policemen stopped me and demanded money. My heart beat faster and my breathing became laboured. I did not know where to turn since I did not have a single shilling. Just then, I saw a Kenyan pastor and waved vigorously at him. He looked at the policemen and knew I was in trouble. He advocated for me and convinced the police to release me.

As I approached my home, I heard someone call my name but did not perceive who. I did not linger because of the police encounter which had traumatized me. I did not want to risk another arrest. A few steps from the door, the individual caught up to me and pushed an envelope into my hands, "I am sorry I could not bring this sooner. I was impressed to give it to you a week ago but was busy and did not have time to find you." The woman's words surprised me. I mumbled a confused "thank you" and she disappeared quickly into a small crowd of people.

My cousins and I were curious but also anxious to see the contents of the envelope. We had heard of cases where people had been hospitalized after opening envelopes that contained poison. Cautiously, I opened the envelope and discovered a bill for one thousand Ksh. Although I was sure Hope Africa University would not accept this little amount (thirty-three thousand Ksh was required), I was determined to give it a try. I reminded myself that this was an opportunity to practice my new discipline of faith.

I headed to school the next day with a grain of faith. I told the accountant about the gift of money and he brushed me off, thinking it was a joke. I did not let his response faze me, determined to use the money for school fees and nothing else. This was what I had been praying and fasting for!

I proceeded to the finance manager's office but Mr. Lúbunga's response was the same. I left his office in desperation and went to a nearby tree to take a deep breath and pray. In the middle of my prayer, Mr. Lúbunga called my name. "I have been disturbed since you left my office. I will accept your money and allow you to attend class." He issued a receipt that read, "1,000 Ksh and the remaining 32,000 in pledge."

My English vocabulary was still poor so I had to run to the library to find out what "pledge" meant. I bounded to the registrar's office with my receipt, drunk with excitement. The registrar was not happy to see the meagre amount but he could not overturn the finance manager's decision. I started class that day and soaked up every word and concept like a sponge — I was finally studying! I pranced home after class, reflecting on how much faith, optimism and prayer can make a difference.

During that semester, I happily accepted a work assignment to help pay off thirty percent of the remaining "pledge." Before long, I had successfully completed my first year of university studies. I also received a mandate letter from the UNHCR accepting me as a refugee in Kenya, but the letter stated I must reside in the refugee camp in Kakuma. I refused, willing to risk apprehension instead of being robbed of the opportunity to advance my education.

I was informed that Hope Africa University was relocating to Burundi in January 2004: it was not allowed to continue in Kenya due to government regulations. I knew I could excel in Burundi since the program would be delivered in French, but I simply did not have the resources to travel to a new country, let alone manage the cost of living and ongoing school fees. My studies had come to an abrupt halt.

In January 2004, my cousin Joseph packed his luggage and left for Burundi, with funding through an American friend of his family. My cousin's wife and two children did not accompany him because of concern over sustained violence between the government and rebels there.

I had no choice but to stay in Nairobi. I did not know what to do with my life, yet trusted I would somehow fulfill my educational dreams. Joseph's wife Maùwa, their two children and I moved back to my Uncle's cramped, two-room apartment in Githurai 45. I slept on the couch in the sitting room and my two cousins slept on the floor beside me. The apartment was over-crowded but I was grateful to have a place to live.

In mid-January 2004, I started a six-month computer program at Faraja College through the support of the Sisters of Saint Francis (a Catholic mission that offered different services for refugees). I felt productive even though it was not exactly what I wanted to study. After obtaining a certificate, I worked as a secretary, typing and editing papers on computer for my Uncle. He was completing his undergraduate degree at Pan Africa Christian University.

I could not let my educational dream die! Through contributions from James of the Full Gospel Church, Pastor Rukukuye, Christ Ambassadors' Fellowship (a ministry by refugees from DR Congo, Burundi and Rwanda) and friends and family, I managed to raise $500 US. This would pay for the necessary paperwork to leave the country and assist towards the first semester and living expenses in Burundi.

Little did I anticipate the perils ahead. I departed for Burundi in September 2004 and was detained at the border by an immigration officer who threatened to put me in jail. After pleading and begging, I was released after paying a bribe of one thousand five hundred Ksh. Shortly after my release by the Kenyan police, I was stopped by Ugandan police. It took considerable explanation, negotiation and bribing to pass the first two borders but thankfully I had no problem at the Rwandan border. By the time I arrived in Kigali, the capital of Rwanda, it was late and I had to spend the night in a hotel. The next day I embarked on the final leg of the journey to Burundi, ambivalent to danger ahead.

Rwanda is called the "land of a thousand hills" for good reason. The minivan I was riding in traveled through the hilly country at breakneck speed, arriving at the Rwanda-Burundi border before I knew it. After being cleared to proceed, the minivan sped off. While turning on a steep incline, a side door of the minivan suddenly flung open and two passengers were expelled, while I screamed and held on for dear life. Apparently, a guard at the border inspection had left the door unlatched without anyone noticing. The two were critically injured and rushed to the nearest health centre. After that, I did not want to return to the same seat but no one was willing to exchange with me. The conductor reassured me the door was closed but my nerves were frayed from this near death experience.

"It is a miracle you are still with us."

I did not know what to expect in Burundi. My cousin Joseph had warned me repeatedly about shootings at night. I boldly proclaimed I was not worried. It was not until the shootings started in early evening that I realized it was a serious concern. Within moments, I too became petrified and sought a place to hide. At first the shooting seemed far away but soon gunshots sounded in our neighbourhood. Fire from the bombs and gunshots lit up the sky above our residence. I had never expected to live among gunfire again.

I had lived with shootings in DR Congo and yet I was horror-struck at the violence in this new city. I worried about bloodshed from deadly clashes between rebels and the government. Reports indicated people were being killed day and night, which revived horrific memories from DR Congo. Many of my Kenyan friends had never experienced such intense shootings and were very frightened. Some even began to pack their luggage to return home. Unlike my Kenyan friends, I had nowhere safe to go.

My whole life was constantly changing with no place to

call home. I longed to be like others who could live peacefully in their motherland. Growing up, I had become so attached to my homeland — the lake, hills, fauna and flora that graced my village and country — but the brutality and greed of man had refused to let me float peacefully on the waters of precious Lake Tanganyika. In this predicament, I had to rely on my God to save me.

When it came time for my first meal at the university, I realized my name was not on the list but I was served on condition of payment the next day. We ate rice with *ndagaa* (small fish from Lake Tanganyika) and beans mixed together, a combination that I had never tried before. It was amazing to eat fish again after going so long without it. After the meal, Joseph introduced me to other Congolese men. Many assumed I was rich since I came from Nairobi. Little did they know of my desperate financial situation with dwindling means to pay for the meal I had just eaten.

The next morning we observed the school's very first graduation of less than sixty students. It was a joyous occasion as family, graduates and staff celebrated this milestone. Afterwards, Joseph showed me around the downtown of Bujumbura. I noted the heavily armed police and soldiers on almost every corner but it appeared they did not arrest people at random, as in Nairobi.

Before heading back to the residence, my cousin took me to try Burundian milk, often referred to as *amata meza* (fresh milk from local cows). As I sipped the delicious yogurt-like milk, I reminisced of life in Lusenda. My family had some cows and we were allotted two litres of fresh milk per week. I remembered fighting with my sisters over milk since there was not enough for everyone.

It was the first time I could pay most of the term fees at the time of registration. I felt indebted to all the people in Kenya who generously gave towards my studies. I wanted to send them an email to express my appreciation but discovered I could not afford internet services.

Despite shootings almost every night, the first semester kicked off well. I began my second year in Burundi but was still one semester behind my friends who had come in February. I was determined to catch up by doing intensive and summer courses, although I didn't know where the finances would come from.

Despite the stress of adjustment, I successfully completed the semester, earning my highest Grade Point Average (GPA) yet. I guess eating mikeke, my favourite fish from Lake Tanganyika, boosted my immune system and intelligence. After exams, most students went home to celebrate Christmas with their families, except a few of us who had nowhere to go. I could not risk returning to DR Congo nor could I afford to visit my family in Nyarugusu refugee camp. The school graciously allowed us to stay on campus but we needed to arrange our own meals. I had already survived without food for days so I knew it would not be my demise.

January 2005 came and it was time to register for an intensive two-week course. I had scrimped and saved enough to pay half the fee, allowing me to attend class and stay in residence. Meanwhile, I aggressively hunted for finances to continue my studies. Joseph and Asúla gave me a little money which I used to pay for internet time to apply online for scholarships.

As I prayerfully waited and waited for a response, I recalled the many times when the needs of my sisters and I were met by random strangers while begging in DR Congo. Moreover, completing high school in Nyarugusu refugee camp and surviving death multiple times convinced me that my life had a greater purpose, despite uncontrollable circumstances that threatened to crush me.

I avoided the first day of registration by meditating, fasting and praying for an answer. The next day I mustered the courage to enter the registrar's office. The accountant from Nairobi was now the finance manager. I expected another "get out of my office" response since he knew my financial situation. I had become all too familiar with that English phrase from the start of my studies.

To this day, I can clearly remember his unexpected smile and declaration, "Someone from the United States has volunteered to pay for the rest of your education at Hope Africa University." I stared at him dumbfounded and asked, "Did I hear you well?" He repeated, "Someone has volunteered to pay for the rest of your education." Immediately I sprung from my seat, jumping around his office like a child who had just won a prize.

I could not contain my exuberant joy and hugged him several times while thanking him, the school and the stranger who had extended special grace to me. As the finance manager processed the registration forms, my Grandpa's words rang out loud and clear, "Struggle is part of the human condition. It does not have to be wasted out of fear or to seek control in a seemingly uncontrollable situation. Perhaps struggle is the most important miracle that the Creator will give you to achieve your life purpose. Embrace life with courage and determination to never give up."

This day marked the beginning of a life transformed by an extraordinary man on the other side of the world. This man may have seemed average to many but he was outstanding to me because he cared enough to help a stranger across the globe. My registration form was signed, "US sponsor" and I was given an extra $15 US for pocket money each month.

Even though it was late, I bought milk and bread and went to Joseph's household to share the incredible news. We rejoiced together, recounting and joking about the many times I had been told "get out of my office" due to lack of money. Prayer and fasting had produced fruit in my life!

School infrastructure was lacking and while dormitory construction was underway, the school rented a big house to accommodate about fifty students. Bunk beds were spread all over and two people had to share a twin bed, with eight in each room, leaving minimal space for anything else. At times we had no electricity for hours or days, forcing us to study by candlelight. I remember many times lighting two candles, one on the left and another on the right side of my chair. However, this inconvenience did not compare to my previous stress over lack of finances. Now that my school fees were guaranteed, I saw no further obstacle to becoming a Social Worker – a degree that I knew would enable me to transform lives.

Through the support of many Western sponsors, the new dorms were completed and an inaugural service was held, attended by government dignitaries and donors from the United States and other parts of the world. In 2006, I was elected as a member of the student council and was put in charge of spiritual and social affairs. I found joy and contentment in working with people from different nationalities. Since the school was bilingual (French and English), I interpreted in chapel every week, as well as led praise and worship. I also revived the campus fellowship and served as the Bible group secretary. My involvement in these activities gained me a certain degree of popularity and I was able to encourage and inspire students at every level of study.

I often reflected on Burundi's situation: A country torn apart by war before independence and continued oppression after, with the minority Tutsi ethnic group ruling the country for decades. Now, the Hutus, the majority group in the country, were fighting for balance of power. Hope Africa University was led by the late Bishop Dr. Elie, a Hutu who himself had been in exile for many years. He was an active citizen both in the political and church arena.

Many of my professors were also Hutus who had been in exile for years and were now returning to work for their country as negotiations between the Hutu rebels and Tutsi-led government took place in Tanzania. After listening to them, it became clear that through education, the son of a miner could become a manager, the daughter of a peasant could become a doctor and the child of a farmer could become a social worker, activist and great leader. This knowledge gave me a vision for my beloved Congo: positive change can happen through education and hope can be restored.

# 16

# CONNECTIONS

How could I know that a budding friendship with Westerners would change the trajectory of my life in a dramatic way? I first met Bob and Laurie Hughes, North American missionaries, when I was asked to interpret for them. Later, when they moved on campus to work in different capacities, our friendship grew and in 2006, I began helping around their house.

I treasured working for them because they treated me as a son and after all I had been through, it was therapeutic to have a sense of belonging. They were the father and mother figure I so badly needed; rich in love, irrespective of race or colour. After I finished house chores, Laurie often invited me to bake with her while Bob graded papers or did repairs about the house. Laurie was loving, kind and generous, often sending fresh baked goods home with me.

I eagerly participated in daily activities with Bob and

Laurie. By spending time with them, I learned a lot about life in North America and its culture. They would often invite me for dinner or take me shopping. It was my first time to shop in some of the better stores in Burundi, knowing only second hand stores on a student budget. I came to meet almost every American that visited Hope Africa University through Bob and Laurie, who introduced me as their African son. Laurie (now deceased) hoped that one day I would visit their home in Wenatchee, a city in the United States.

By the end of 2006, I had finished my social work placement by working with street kids at Don Bosco Buterere. These placement hours would count towards accreditation in a distant land in the future, although I did not know it at the time. It was an enriching placement as it allowed me to reflect on my own experiences and learn about the therapeutic use of self in social work practice. After a day at the centre, I would come home encouraged that my life had started to bear fruit and that past experiences during the war now enabled me to empathize with others.

To finish my social work degree in Burundi, I had to write a thesis. I chose to develop a personal approach towards counselling in response to the unmet expectations of HIV/AIDS patients from Prince Regent Charles Hospital, one of the country's largest public hospitals. The number of HIV/AIDS patients was growing in Burundi but patients lacked psychosocial support from medical personnel.

It was my first time to witness how HIV/AIDS was rampant and destroying lives. I spent hours listening to stories from patients who were devastated by this condition, being robbed of everything they had — from health to finances to family and friends. Children were becoming orphans and widows had no hope of inheriting anything in a patriarchal culture. Many times I was paralyzed by the lack of resources and felt like a failure due to my inability to defend the oppressed — something I strongly believed in. The system appeared corrupt and burdened and no one seemed to care, but it was encouraging when some cases made the news, sparking action from international organizations to provide much-needed resources.

I was counting the days to the finish line at university. In February 2007, I defended my thesis in a room packed with over sixty people, leaving only standing room for some. Even more people stood outside, watching and listening through the open windows. After my twenty-minute exposition, it was time for questions from the panel followed by a few from the audience. Before any questions, my thesis supervisor, Jerome, turned to the audience and commented, "It was good for me to supervise someone who is determined, committed and focused." He praised my time management skills and positive attitude toward learning. I was thrilled to hear his comments. He asked a few questions that I answered with confidence and then he passed the microphone to the other panel members. After everyone on the panel had asked their questions, anyone in the audience with an undergraduate degree could ask a question. Only one person had a question and it was simple to answer.

The room erupted in shouts of joy when an "A" grade was declared. Everyone was proud of my academic milestone. I was mounted on the shoulders of fellow students and carried across campus, like a victory march after battle. I rejoiced knowing I had completed my undergraduate degree and would soon be a Social Worker. My relative, Asúla (now deceased), had arranged a small party where friends and family joined us for light refreshments.

I remembered the struggles and traumatic events that had sharpened my character, built resilience and taught me to be thankful. How blessed I was. Looking back, the most difficult experiences in my life had turned into opportunities for growth and character development. On the other hand, I did not understand why traumatic recollections would resurface every time I celebrated a milestone, until I discovered that I needed to continue to reconcile my past with the present.

I had to move off campus after May 2007 since I had completed my studies. This spun me into another dilemma. I did not have a stable source of income, although I was able to earn a little by teaching computer courses part-time. Money was also tight because I hoped to visit my family in Nyarugusu refugee camp in Tanzania in July. I knew that my absence was emotionally taxing on my family, using mail as the only means of communication.

City life taught me about a structured postal system. Back in my village we would wave down a bus heading in the desired direction and hand our letter to one of the travelers. This person would deliver the mail to another, who would in turn get it to the right person. Sometimes the bus would not stop at the designated village so the mail would be thrown out the window with a shout to whoever was within earshot to deliver it. Unlike my village, people in Nairobi did not seem to know each other. *I guess this is why they need a postal system*, I mused.

One evening, Bob and Laurie invited me to their place for dinner to meet Professor Paul and his wife Carol, who would soon return to the United States. Laurie introduced me as their African son and briefly shared my story, proudly telling them about my upcoming graduation and trip to Nyarugusu refugee camp. The two visitors were very curious about life in the camp and how I would get there. They could not believe that I would have to take a taxi bike for approximately five hundred kilometres, half of the journey.

It was a well-spent evening and new friendships were formed. Paul and Carol requested I accompany them to their guest room on campus and we chatted another hour. On my way out, they gave me their contact information and ten thousand Burundi Francs for the road, praying for travelling mercies. I was again amazed how strangers had poured their love and support into my life.

During my studies, a friendship with a lady began to flourish, despite our different interests, personalities and worldviews. I lived by principles of simplicity and she was the opposite. However, we focused on helping others, hospitality, traveling and agreed on the importance of family. We spent hours cooking together while talking about ways to change the world, especially how we could use our education to advocate for better policies in DR Congo and beyond.

She was passionate about using her law degree to help others and I saw many links between social work and law. I firmly believed that these two disciplines would make a perfect match to address the injustices in our homeland — rape, robbery, land exploitation and murder, to name only a few. Many other couples on campus envied us and were excited about the plans we had for the world and ourselves. Together we believed that we could advocate for policies that respected human dignity.

My girlfriend left to be with her family in Uvira for the holidays. Two days before leaving, she introduced me to her parents and two brothers who came to visit her. My impression was that her father was a good man who worked hard to provide for his family. Despite the impact of war on his business, he was able to keep his farm and bought and sold minerals as well. He introduced me to the precious metal called coltan, an essential metal in electronic devices and other technology. Years later, I would discover that world demand for coltan had escalated greed, leading to the exploitation of resources, murder and oppression in the eastern Congo.

The next day I woke up early to catch a mini bus to Sosumo, a Burundian village close to the Tanzanian border. Upon arrival, taxi bikes from Nyarugusu refugee camp were already waiting for passengers. I was astonished to see one of my fellow high school graduates as a taxi driver and quickly gave him my business. Time flew by as we journeyed, talking about our lives since high school graduation. He looked weary and aged, revealing the visible toll that life in Nyarugusu refugee camp had on him. He explained that he had taken up this job to support his wife and five children, then shared his grief over losing two of his children to malaria. I was in tears over the things he had to endure in the camp.

I arrived mid-afternoon in Nyarugusu refugee camp and roused my young sister Evelyn from her nap. At first she looked as if she had seen a ghost but then recognized me and ran overjoyed to the tent to tell everyone. My whole family came to hug me — it had been so long since I had seen them. My sister Mapenzi (who was six when the war broke out in 1996) had grown so much that I almost didn't recognize her. I brought fish, bread, fruit and sugar and she ran to light the firewood to make a meal for everyone. There was a lot to catch up on.

Although I was happy to be back, I felt a sense of guilt at the sight of my family and friends living in such poor circumstances. I knew there was little I could do at this time but I was confident I had chosen my path correctly. By taking the risk to leave and pursue higher education, I would someday help in tangible and significant ways.

Night came quickly and I stayed with my cousin Lúala. We had shared a tent and bed during my five years in the camp. He was still hoping to complete high school, having taken the national exam a few times without success. I had spent more time with him than anyone else in the camp — fishing, swimming, mushroom picking and cutting bamboo together. I was overjoyed to see him and it was well past midnight when we finally stopped talking.

My two weeks in Nyarugusu refugee camp were very emotional. I could not stop crying over the struggles of my people, who were now deemed Congolese refugees. My former high school friends had three to five children, many of whom were malnourished. I wanted to escape this harsh reality and return to Bujumbura where life was more than subsistence but I knew that I should do something before leaving.

I spent the next week teaching the basics of crisis and trauma intervention, based on courses I had taken at Hope Africa University. I was not an expert but I was eager to make a difference. I also offered counselling sessions to many individuals. Although I had majored in social work and community development, I was blessed to have a minor in counselling. In my sessions, I drew from all the courses and experiences of my undergraduate program. Counselling was new to the people and I had to find strategic ways to present concepts to them. As much as specific approaches helped, I think most of my success came from basic soft skills: warmth, genuineness, empathy and acceptance.

There was much more that needed to be done to help my fellow Congolese in Nyarugusu refugee camp, but it was time for me to return to Burundi. In my heart I knew my work was not finished. I would find a way to tell the world about the plight of the Congolese. I was determined to improve their situation in the camp and in DR Congo. I was so focused on this purpose that I did not notice the warning signs of impending betrayal.

Some of my family including my Mother and I in Nyarugusu Camp, 1998

Nyarugusu Tents

The Samburu Youth with Oliver after a Daniel Poultry Project meeting, 2010

My parents and I, before I left for Canada, 201

Bill and Marilyn welcome my arrival to Canada, 2011

Oliver and Miriam's wedding, 2013

STILL WITH US

Miriam and I in Nyarugusu Refugee Camp, 2014

Participants of the seminar led by Msenwa when he returned to Nyarugusu Camp, 2014

My MSW graduation at University of Waterloo, 2014

# 17

# BETRAYAL

I welcomed 2008 with fervour and optimism, birthing new resolutions and aspirations. Life was busy between work in the academic secretary's office, teaching at a local high school, helping my American family with household chores and planning for the future with my girlfriend. At the end of February I proposed to her and was elated when she accepted.

I started making plans to raise funds for a dowry as required by our culture. I began saving every penny, denying myself the pleasure of going out. I dreamed about our life together and wanted to be wed within the year. We had not decided where we would live, knowing it was not an option to return to DR Congo and there was no future in Nyarugusu refugee camp.

In July 2008, I began cataloguing work in the library, as taught by Laurie who was like a mother to me. Around the same time, my relative Asúla confirmed my intentions to marry and in **August**, my Father came from the refugee camp to collect my savings and travel to DR Congo to pay the dowry to my fiancée's parents. Between my savings and contributions from my parents and a few friends in the United States, I had raised $2,100 US dollars.

My family was astounded at the amount I was able to raise and my Father confidently went to DR Congo to present the dowry. Unexpectedly, my fiancée's father demanded $3,000 US dollars, an enormous amount since it was ten times the annual wage of someone in DR Congo. An agreement was reached after an additional $350 was presented the next day from my cousin in Lusenda and I pledged to raise the remaining funds. With that great sum of money, permission was granted to move ahead with plans for a December wedding.

I planned to raise the remaining funds by drafting project proposals for an international organization. I had taken a class on proposals in my third year and written some for another organization. When these proposals were funded, news spread and partner organizations approached me to draft more.

Two days after my Father had paid the enormous dowry, rumours began to circulate that my fiancée was not always where she claimed to be, but love blinded me from investigating the truth. I trusted her so much that I could not disbelieve anything she said. Others knew the truth but wouldn't disclose it for fear of hurting my feelings. My cousin Joseph didn't tell me that he had heard from a trustworthy source that my fiancée had been seen going out with another man, someone she knew from high school. I later learned this had been going on for several months.

One day I attempted to call my fiancée several times but she didn't answer her phone and another two days passed without seeing each other. "I don't understand what is going on with her?" I confided to Joseph. He hesitated, then spoke, "Brother, I know you are deeply in love with her. I don't want to be the one to break your heart with bad news." My heart began to beat faster and I prodded, "Since when did we start hiding things from each other?"

He remained hesitant but I persisted, "I have done social work and can manage my emotions well. You know everything else I have gone through, Joseph — from war to begging on the streets, hopelessness in Nyarugusu, going nowhere in Nairobi and even escaping death — there is nothing I can't handle." Although I was putting up a good facade, inside my heart was not ready for another traumatic event now that life seemed to be heading in the right direction. Of all the things I had lost in life, I was not ready to lose a relationship that seemed to be the only thing that was stable.

I could not believe what my cousin disclosed in the next few minutes. My engagement was shattered, learning my fiancée had chosen another to be her life partner, possibly because her mother did not want her to marry a man from outside their tribe. I was perplexed that nothing in my life seemed to remain constant. I was left alone in my apartment, crying and cursing the day I met this woman.

In the midst of my turmoil, I still held on to false hope that everything I had heard was untrue. I went to work but I couldn't concentrate, not wanting others to know about the relationship breakdown. I gathered the courage to disclose my turmoil to Laurie over cookies at break. She was astonished but empathic. Through verbalization, the truth began to sink in like a dead weight: my fiancée had rejected me, no longer interested in returning my messages or spending time with me. I had invested so much in the relationship and felt like a failure. I lost weight from the internal torment and a broken heart. Promises were unfulfilled.

Days later, after processing the truth, my fiancée approached me as if nothing was wrong. When I questioned her whereabouts, she was evasive and came up with a lame excuse for not being around. She denied all implications of seeing another man and demanded tangible proof, knowing I could demand the return of dowry money if she was proven guilty of causing the relationship to fail.

I quickly learned that I was dealing with a law student who needed evidence for everything. I needed a strategy to ensure others didn't think I ended the relationship, for the sake of reclaiming my dowry and reputation. Despite the emotional upheaval, I resolved to remain calm as I pondered my next steps. I asked myself, *Where I can get more information to deal with this? Whom can I consult? How can I transform this ruin into opportunity? What would my hero, Grandpa Msenwa do?*

Grandpa Msenwa had passed away in Nyarugusu refugee camp in 2005 and I could not attend his burial due to lack of money for the trip. I missed him and his words of wisdom so acutely. In the meantime, I needed to avoid the victim mentality. In faith, I accepted the situation as it came and sought support from friends and family. Others shared how I was not alone in experiencing hurt from relationship breakdown. As painful as it was, I was determined to move forward with my life.

I gathered evidence of my former fiancée's flirtatious indiscretions with another man, aided by spies working on my behalf. Photos were taken of her at various parties and other locations, but she still denied everything. At one point, she showed up at my apartment and boldly started searching for the photos which were evidence. Fortunately my friends were able to get her out while I simmered with intense rage, resolving not to retaliate in aggression.

I wondered about the abrupt change in this woman I had considered making a life partner. Her countenance and character had completely changed, turning into a stranger I had never known. I held several negotiations with her father but open-mindedness was lacking and the dowry money was not returned to my Father.

I thought we loved each other since the beginning of our relationship until I came to discover that it is not emotions that sustain a relationship but the decision to love despite fleeting emotions. I could not believe that her love for me was merely an infatuation that vanished so quickly. I painfully learned that when two people choose to make things work, love is a choice — not an emotion. I learned that an unwavering commitment to love despite shifting emotions is what produces a long-lasting and respectful relationship.

I felt ashamed as word spread about our break up and I started receiving messages of condolence from others at school. It was then that I realized I had lost something: the dream of a life partner. Betrayal was overwhelming and I became cautious in my future dealings with women. With strong convictions, I believed I would someday find the woman of my dreams: a woman with patience, kindness, goodness, generosity, gentleness, modesty, self-control and chastity.

# 18

# DISTANT PROSPECT

Singleness was not what I wanted but it proved to be a blessing. Unexpectedly, I was asked if I would like to immigrate to Canada. This question came in an email from Professor Paul who was now back in the United States. Apparently, a Canadian family was willing to help my friend John immigrate to Canada but they insisted there must be another "single" male refugee to include in the process. Finding a safe, permanent country would provide stability and could open doors to help others, but I was not in the right state of mind to accept this opportunity. During a phase of dejection, my friend John came to beg me to respond to the email and confirm that I would be interested.

A week later in October 2008, I acquiesced. Leaving Burundi would be healthy emotionally but I did not want people to think I ran away because of the betrayal. Professor Paul connected me by email to the Canadian family that was willing to facilitate the process. In their first email, I was bombarded with a multitude of questions ranging from my relationship status, level of education, fluency in French and English, work experience and interests. In the exchanged emails, a sense of hope was re-kindled.

I soon realized I had to travel back to Kenya to renew my expired UNHCR document and submit my immigration application to the designated Canadian Embassy, which was in Nairobi. I prepared for the journey to Kenya, planning to use accumulated vacation time. I expected to be back in Burundi for work on January 13, 2009. Little did I know that December 16, 2008 would be my last day in Burundi for many years.

I boarded a crowded bus heading to Uganda. My seat was close to the window since I wanted to enjoy the scenery while reflecting on my last weeks in Burundi. I greeted Jean, the person sitting beside me and discovered he was a fellow Congolese, traveling to Kampala for business purposes. He owned a jewellery and clothing boutique in Uvira but insecurity in DR Congo made it difficult to thrive there. His shop had been attacked three times by armed robbers and everything was stolen.

There was much to discuss with this fellow Congolese who had also lived in Nyarugusu refugee camp but had returned to DR Congo when his father was dying. He had inherited his father's herds and farmland. My fellow traveller had faced several attacks by armed militia, without help from local authorities and he was forced to witness the rape of his wife. I thought I had enough struggles of my own, but I was stunned to hear the unbearable cruelty he had endured. I then shared my life's journey since 1996 when the war broke out. We shared our misery over the invasion of DR Congo by foreign forces, stealing resources and ravaging our land. Revealing our stories brought mutual tears, yet we were encouraged, understanding each other's pain.

A sense of dread washed over me as we arrived at the border of Burundi, recalling the last time I was there in 2004. I remembered the near-fatal accident when two were critically injured after being ejected from the bus. The trauma resurfaced and I feared another dreadful event. Thankfully, we crossed both the Burundi and Rwanda borders safely. By then I was optimistic I would arrive safely in Kenya.

It was dark and I was on my own after arriving in Kampala, Uganda around midnight. I had read about the Ugandan warlord Joseph Kony and his rebels attacking and killing innocent people, especially at night. I had come too far to die at this stage in my life! Spotting a security guard, I mustered up the courage to ask for directions and help to get a bus to Kenya. Despite paranoia, I decided to trust him as he arranged a motorcycle taxi in a language foreign to me. Upon arrival at the bus terminal, I learned the next bus to Nairobi would not leave until morning.

I could not afford a motel so I reluctantly paid one hundred Ksh to be permitted to spend the night inside the terminal. That night was spent with open, watchful eyes, fearing I would be robbed. Mosquitoes feasted on me as I watched Nigerian movies to pass the time. Finally when morning came, I bought a ticket to Nairobi, a four-hour journey.

Once in Nairobi, Kenya, I had to wait until the next morning to take a bus to Githurai 45. On arrival, I was saddened by the dilapidated condition of the building where Joseph's parents still lived. It had no running water and the walls and floors were full of cracks and openings. My cousins Angela, Lucy and Furaha had to fetch water a kilometre away. I was frustrated and angry that the landlord did not care to maintain the living quarters of his tenants.

My utmost priority was to go to the UNHCR office that day, since it would be closed the next day for the holidays. Although exhausted from my trip, I scurried to find an escort to get me there. While on the bus, my escort Chantal shared how Kenya was trying to recover from post-election violence that had resulted in the loss of lives and property. I did not realize how much Kenya had changed since I left.

After the UNHCR security check, I was issued a number and waited three hours before being served. I presented my expired letter to the person at the counter who asked a few questions and then told me to come back on January 22. "Could you please give me an appointment in early January?" I pleaded, but was ignored. I left the office fuming and asking, why did I come back to deal with the UN again?

I wrestled with returning to Burundi in time for work on January 13 or waiting for the UNHCR appointment on January 22, 2009. I knew Burundi was not a permanent or safe place for me because of the violence as well as random encounters with enemies who had wanted my demise in

DR Congo. But, I had made some good friendships and felt at ease there, compared to the alternative. I was so befuddled that I entered the wrong bus and only realized when I reached the end of the route.

My eyes were heavy from sleepless nights as my mind battled for direction. When I arrived at my Uncle's place, he was shocked to see me, especially since he was preparing to go to Burundi for my wedding. I refused to give any explanation until I had rested. I was too physically and emotionally exhausted. The apartment turned into a beehive of activity when everyone arrived home. As I was pelted with questions, my assumption dissolved — coming to Nairobi was not an escape. Their youngest son David, almost seven at that time, blurted out, "Kwani uli kataliwa na bibi, tuambiye bro," literally meaning, "Did the wife divorce you? Just spit it out, bro!" As all eyes turned to me, my mournful eyes divulged a deep inner sorrow. They soon discovered the sad story of betrayal.

I went to an internet cafe to inform my Canadian family that I had arrived safely in Kenya, but that I was uncertain how long the UNHCR process would take. I also needed a place to stay, not because David had made me weep over my shattered relationship but because their house was crowded and I did not want to be a burden. I knew their finances were tight since my Uncle was studying towards a post-graduate degree and his wife was trying to sustain their family on meagre earnings. They obviously could not afford to move from their dilapidated apartment, lacking the five months' advance rent required to secure a place elsewhere.

I longed for security and stability in my life. I could not return to Nyarugusu refugee camp or DR Congo, and Burundi was only a temporary option since I was there illegally and that meant job instability, not to mention the emotional trauma that resurfaced every time I heard shootings. Doors were closing and it seemed right to focus on immigration to Canada since that appeared to be the only viable solution, yet my patience would again be tested beyond measure.

# 19

# PATIENCE TESTED

I anticipated becoming homeless in Kenya. My Uncle's home was already packed and I knew no other relatives that might host me, yet behind the scenes a possibility was emerging. Just before Christmas in 2008, my Canadian contact emailed me and suggested I meet Dr. Kirk, also Canadian and presently the Vice Chancellor of Pan Africa Christian University in Nairobi, Kenya. Although the school was closed for the holidays, he met with me after receiving an appeal from my Canadian contact. Hope rose from deep within when Dr. Kirk indicated I could do some work on campus in exchange for room and board. I left his office jumping for joy, not foreseeing the stressors that awaited me with this work.

I quickly ran to an internet cafe to email my Canadian link about Dr. Kirk's offer. I inquired about the connection with Dr. Kirk and why he was willing to help. I needed shelter for an undetermined period of time, realizing the immigration process could take five or more years. I was fascinated to hear that my Canadian connection had never met Dr. Kirk but their youngest daughter Victoria had gone to a Christian school in the primary grades with Kirk's daughter, Kaitlyn. They had maintained their friendship since these early years. It was through that connection I was now receiving aid.

I marvelled at how events in my life continued to be orchestrated. About twenty-two years ago, I was swinging from my atùcù tree in Lusenda, Congo shouting, "Going to Kenya Nairobi, Kenya Nairobi" and years later, a relationship between two school girls in Canada had provided room and board for me in Kenya as I waited on the immigration process. I could not wait to meet and thank these girls for maintaining a unique friendship that had such a measurable impact on me.

On January 5, 2009 I settled into my new home at Pan Africa Christian University (PACU). The security guard let me enter, understanding I had connections with the "big boss." When Dr. Kirk introduced me to Anataka, the Dean of Students, his eyes lit up as he said, "Je suis Congolais aussi!" We immediately began speaking in animated French. Anataka then introduced me to Shadrach, the Head of Maintenance, who decided the type of work I would do.

I was handed soap and water in a bucket, along with a mop and ordered to clean floors and bathrooms for faculty and students. This was a first and it wasn't until Shadrach corrected my mopping technique that I figured out I did not meet his stern approval. His attitude and comments were demeaning and abrasive. I felt demoralized, realizing I had left a job in Burundi where others had cleaned for me. With a university degree, this job was below my potential and my pride was wounded.

My future was uncertain and rested in the hands of the Canadian immigration system, which offered no guarantee that I would be accepted. I wondered what would happen if at the end of five years, I was not approved to immigrate to Canada: Where would I start life again? How would my friends and family perceive me? Working on campus led nowhere other than providing temporary food and shelter. Through it all, I remained thankful and trusted things would work out.

The day of my appointment with the UNHCR arrived, but I had to clean from 4 a.m. to 6 a.m. because I was still expected to complete my duties on campus. Due to traffic congestion, I did not arrive at the UNHCR office until 9:30 a.m. I passed through the security gate and was assigned a number. I sat beside another Congolese and passed the hours by engaging in conversation about our country's politics. Around 3 p.m. I was called in to hear the official statement, "No one has reviewed your case yet. Come back in two weeks." It was hard to believe their lethargy in renewing one simple document. "Why has my case not been reviewed?" I asked. I was ushered out without the courtesy of an answer. I was annoyed at the whole UNHCR system that had failed me several times already. I left the office gnashing my teeth and wishing I had the power to take them to court.

PACU was a small school of approximately three hundred students and it did not take long to make many friends with staff and students. Dejene from Ethiopia and Salomon from DR Congo, both counselling students, became very good friends. We bonded so well that I spent most of my time with them discussing politics, education, sports, movies and family matters. Dejene was married with two children while Salomon was younger and single, but very mature in his judgment and worldview. I did not tell them I had recently graduated with a social work degree and they, along with many others, could not understand why I was a custodian and not studying. One day Dejene asked, "How come you speak English and understand so many things?" In confidence, I told him I held a social work degree and was at PACU for temporary shelter while waiting to immigrate to Canada.

Starting in January 2009, I kept in touch with my Canadian contact, Marilyn, and we began to work diligently over the course of several months on the complex and detailed immigration application. Sometimes I felt discouraged and did not want to continue with the comprehensive questions. We spent tedious and exacting hours, meticulously gathering the required information. This often triggered painful recollections, having to account for every month of my whereabouts since I had fled DR Congo in 1996. Every time I thought it was complete, Marilyn would notice another incongruity that required correction. My application could be delayed six months or more if immigration needed even one clarifying detail.

I became perplexed and agitated by the lack of response regarding the renewal of my UNHCR refugee status. By the end of February 2009, I had attended three UNHCR appointments and was told each time to come back after "two weeks." I wanted a definite answer but the only song they sang was "two weeks, two weeks."

I went to a fourth appointment in March and was again told to return in "two weeks." I demanded to see a supervisor, refusing to leave until I did. Two burly security guards were called to escort me out of the office, but I refused and gripped a concrete bench with all my might. I lost my temper and loudly proclaimed, "Justice! I want justice!" At this outburst, the supervisor was summoned to resolve the issue. After hearing my plea, I was assured someone in a higher position would review my case. Later, I questioned the truthfulness of his promise.

I consulted with Marilyn by email, who encouraged me to proceed with my immigration application, anticipating the UNHCR confirmation of "active" refugee status would be forthcoming. Early in the morning on March 19, 2009, my friend Dejene and I took the bus to the Canadian Embassy. I threw my sealed application, containing detailed forms, schedules, documents and photos into their mail box because the security guards at the Canadian Embassy in Nairobi, Kenya would not allow me to enter. I believed that the immigration process did not depend on mere paperwork and the decision of immigration officials. Too much had been orchestrated to get me this far!

The Head of Maintenance resented me and did everything possible to make my life miserable at PACU. He disliked the fact that a Congolese was given work over a fellow Kenyan and turned his prejudice into revengeful words. Every time I would finish cleaning an area, he would comment, "Wewe bure kabisa, akuna kitu umefanya" — literally meaning, "You are useless, you have done nothing." I would do everything I could to appease him but things got worse.

When Dr. Kirk was out of the country, I would appear for meals in the cafeteria and be denied food, for days and even weeks at a time, until Dr. Kirk returned. Tribal hatred and prejudice in Kenya took a different form than what I had witnessed in DR Congo, this time forcing me to starve. In desperation, I would email Dr. Kirk who would apologize and try to rectify the dilemma, not understanding how they could deny me food when it was being wasted every day in the cafeteria and the staff knew I was working in exchange for room and board.

When denied food, I was reminded to never take anything for granted. I spent most of those days fasting, praying and meditating — things that were important but that I often neglected when everything was going well. It seemed that I needed an occasional reminder to remain focused and humble. During these times, I continued to thank God for sustaining me.

Despite lack of food, I never missed a day of custodial work, waking up at 4:30 a.m. to ensure classrooms and washrooms were clean and ready for use by 8:30 a.m. I was thankful my parents had demonstrated and instilled in me a strong work ethic at a formative age.

My friends Dejene and Salomon graciously shared their plates of food with me. One of the kitchen staff was also my friend and sympathetically put more food on my friends' plates, knowing my need. In all this, more than ever, I discovered the value of sharing and the impact it has on someone's life!

By July 2009, discouragement settled in. I had been going to UNHCR appointments every two weeks and was deferred without fail. To top it off, I was still waiting for confirmation that the Canadian Embassy had received my application. Many times I thought of going back to Burundi, but I knew I had already lost my job since I had been absent six months.

Life was stagnant but I was determined to use this situation as an opportunity to overcome adversity. Over and over, I had discovered that emotional resilience was only developed by rising above difficulties. It was not an easy journey but I remembered my Grandpa Msenwa encouraging me to embrace every manner of adversity with calmness, emotional steadiness and patience. Little did I know that in the midst of my struggles, God was making a way where there seemed to be no way.

# 20

# FINDING STRENGTH

During erratic periods of food deprivation on campus, a ray of hope entered my soul. I received an email from my Canadian contact, Marilyn, indicating there was a sponsor who would provide funds for me to enrol in a Master's program at PACU, so I could be productive while waiting to immigrate to Canada. PACU offered a Master's in Leadership with three main streams — business, education and Christian ministries. I jumped for joy, oblivious to those around me in the computer lab. I could not believe that again, someone I did not know would choose to take away my misery. I wondered why some people chose a path of love and generosity while others did not? Deep down in my heart, I told myself that grace-giving as well as grace-receiving would become a priority in my life.

    I left the computer lab and skipped to my friends' place to share the news. We rejoiced together, dancing to Congolese music and thanking God for his provision. The next day I went to the registrar's office to inquire about the program. I was relieved that I had completed my undergraduate degree with a GPA above 3.00, as this was a key requirement for entrance into the Master's program. On my way out, I picked up the application form as the receptionist stared at me in disbelief and declared, "No way! You are just a cleaner!" The LORD was the "lifter of my head" as the Psalmist proclaimed.

I diligently completed the Master's entrance application, including the seven-page essay. I eagerly awaited a response, knowing this was an extraordinary opportunity. With the arrival of my letter of acceptance, I was advised to start studies on December 19, 2009 with an intensive two-week course on "Foundations of Leadership." I longed for that day when I would again set foot in a classroom — not to clean but to immerse myself in learning.

I had dreamed of continuing my education one day but my parents were still living in the refugee camp and I was cleaning toilets, with no money to pay for basic necessities, let alone a Master's degree. I realized in that moment that I had been harbouring bitterness and self-pity. I felt energized and motivated to push my struggles aside as I recalled my Grandpa's words: "Many people start the race but only a few persevere to the finish line. I want you to finish, *mashina* (friend)."

I joyfully bounded to my first class consisting of students from Kenya, Ethiopia, Tanzania, Uganda and DR Congo. I was thrilled Dr. Kirk had relieved me of cleaning responsibilities during that two-week course, but worried about my source of food. I formed friendships with Phillip from Tanzania, Weston from Kenya (who had lived in the United States for seven years) and Oselu, another Kenyan. They generously shared their food and assisted me in writing academic papers according to a new format. By the end of this course, I had acquired new skills and made many connections within our multicultural classroom.

When school closed for the Christmas holidays, I was invited to the hometown of a friend from Samburu. We spent one week in his village helping the Masaai youth. This opened my eyes to the local poverty and hopelessness. Their situation was a reminder of my life in Nyarugusu refugee camp. I cried over the many naked and malnourished children there. The region was semi-arid and drought made it hard for people to grow crops. I also learned that female genital mutilation was being practiced, causing infection and death in young girls. Some would run away in order to avoid the trauma associated with the practice.

Overwhelmed by the poverty, I went on a discovery journey with the Masaai youth in Samburu to identify what could be done to inspire hope. Again and again, I heard that education was the greatest need since many dropped out of school due to lack of finances. At the end of my time there, I decided to establish a poultry project which could become a source of income to pay educational fees for youth. I left with a hopeful idea but no capital to fund it.

In faith, I started working on a proposal for the poultry project. I then shared my proposal with Bill and Marilyn in Canada who said their extended family wanted to give towards a special project this Christmas, forfeiting gift-giving to each other. Once again, I could not contain my joy that distant strangers would opt to help desperate youth in Samburu. Hence, the "Daniel Poultry Project" had funding to construct a poultry house and purchase twenty laying hens and food. I felt honoured to provide psychosocial intervention to at-risk youth, including girls that had suffered female genital mutilation. I had dreamed of empowering others and this was a transformational experience I would not trade for anything.

Working with the Samburu youth was a new adventure that forced me to think outside the box. I was previously unaware of female genital mutilation and had no experience in this area of counselling. I embraced every case as a unique opportunity to learn about their culture in a non-judgmental way. Coming from a culture that did not practice female genital mutilation, I tried to avoid making general assumptions and instead, inquisitively and genuinely supported the youth and their families. Many of the elders became accepting when they discovered I was not attempting to force my values on them but instead, desired to work together to find ways to help their youth.

I returned to Nairobi to continue my custodial chores as I waited for the next course to start. I also continued as a volunteer with Christ Ambassador Fellowship where I provided individual and group counselling to survivors of the Congo and Burundi wars. This fellowship was formed by refugees from the Great Lakes region of Africa to provide support to traumatized victims. Working with other survivors made me realize how my life had been affected by war, while enabling me to discover strengths and skills necessary to overcome adversity.

The next Master's course on "Cross Cultural Leadership" intimidated me because it was offered online. It started well, however there was a lot to learn about the software platform. With heavy drought in Kenya, electricity fluctuated on and off, greatly impacting internet connectivity. To cope with overwhelming frustration, I recounted my many blessings, including continued funding if I successfully completed this course. I was also grateful for the renewal of my refugee status by the UNHCR after a year of frustrating and recurring appointments.

The Canadian Embassy sent me a confirmation letter in April 2010, a year after my application was submitted. I feared the approval process could take fifty-four months, as the immigration website indicated, especially after learning that Dr. Kirk was leaving PACU for a new position in Indonesia. I knew my job, in exchange for room and board, would come to an abrupt end at his departure. I started looking for a place off campus, although I did not have rent money. I felt tormented by fear and had to counter that by resting in the knowledge of God's unfailing love and goodness.

In faith, I moved off campus in August 2010 although I did not have a guaranteed source of income. Through the support of various friends and some funds from Canada, I managed to raise money to cover first and last month's rent and my classmate Phillip helped me financially whenever he could, as well as Wachu and Oselu, who each promised to contribute one thousand Kenyan Shillings monthly (about $12 USD).

While I was desperately looking for a bed and other household items, my cousin Ndanga was leaving at the end of July to immigrate with his family to the United States. He offered, "Come to my house and take anything that would be of use to you." I could not believe the timing of this news. I was excited for him and very glad to find a bed and household items for myself. With many others providing sporadic support, I was able to settle into my new place and invite Wachu and Philip for lunch every time they came to campus for a course.

I kept on working with the youth in Samburu and checked on the poultry project. With additional support from Canadian donors, we expanded the project and by the end of 2010 it was able to provide financial support to one high school student. I was very encouraged to see a life changed and to know that several children were also receiving weekly eggs for nourishment.

Life in Nairobi was uneasy, having to depend on the goodwill of others for food and shelter, coupled by a soaring rate of refugee arrests. This created a terrible equation, despite my progress in the two-year Master's program, with only two courses and a thesis left. I had already been arrested on the street several times on my way to or from school. Many policemen wanted bribe money and did not care to see my refugee document. I lacked stability and lived in trepidation.

The call from the Canadian Embassy finally came. I informed my family in Nyarugusu refugee camp, my Canadian sponsors and all my friends about the upcoming interview in March 2011, almost two years since I had submitted my application. Day after day, I prepared myself for the interview, gathering all the required supporting documentation while trying to complete course assignments.

I arrived hours before my interview at the Canadian Embassy on March 15, 2011. It was an intense hour-long interview that focused on my reasons for leaving DR Congo and why I feared for my life and could not return. I responded to all the questions although many of them triggered flashbacks of horrifying memories. At the end of the interview their decision was not disclosed, although I was asked to sign a document, which I later learned was a loan agreement.

My patience was tested again, realizing there was no short cut in the immigration process. A month later, I received a call from the "International Organization for Migration" (IOM) requesting a complete medical check in May 2011, a necessary step in the immigration process. This confused me because the Canadian Embassy had not yet confirmed approval to immigrate. The intense physical assessment included blood and urine testing and tuberculosis screening, taking up most of a day.

I finally received confirmation I was going to Canada when the IOM called me to attend three days of cultural orientation, the last step in the immigration process. The workshop attempted to orientate participants to the Canadian culture and way of life. At the end of the workshop, part of me wondered if I was ready to leave my culture, people and everything familiar. I recalled the many times I had climbed the atùcù and mango and avocado trees in my village. Could I adapt to the cold winters? Would anyone in Canada speak my African languages? Would I see my loved ones again? In recalling my Grandpa's prophecy that I would go to a far away land, I had to believe this was a necessary step in order to fulfill my life purpose and be better positioned to empower those I was leaving behind.

Final details were completed with Immigration Canada, including immunizations and a permanent resident document as a bona fide refugee. I also received approval to complete my last Master's course online as an "independent course" since I had no idea when I would be leaving for Canada. With financial help from others, my parents were able to come from the camp in Tanzania to Kenya for a final farewell. It was a time filled with joy and sadness. My parents were confident it was best for their son but anxious about being so far apart. After ten days together, I wept as my parents returned to the misery in Nyarugusu refugee camp.

I received confirmation that I would travel to Canada on September 27, 2011. I spent my last days in Nairobi visiting friends while trying to prepare myself for life in Canada. Many nights were spent wrestling with thoughts about life in a vastly different country and culture. Taking all my worldly possessions in two suitcases, I bid farewell to the people I cherished and headed to the airport. I was instructed by IOM to arrive early that morning. I wondered why, as my flight to London was scheduled for 11 p.m. which meant I would wait the entire day without food. The reception area was packed with over a hundred people immigrating to different countries around the world.

After being transported from the reception area to the airport, I was given an IOM travel bag containing travel documents, the results of medical tests and a sealed envelope which I was strictly instructed not to open. The sealed envelope was to be given to the immigration officer at the port of entry into Canada. I held it close to my heart, ensuring no one would steal it.

After passing through security, I looked about in curiosity and amazement at how many people were traveling that night. I wondered how they could afford to fly since it seemed quite expensive to me. I also wondered how I would pay my own flight, since I had signed a loan agreement to repay the Canadian government for it. I was shocked by the price of things at the airport, seeing items quadruple the price compared to where I had shopped in Nairobi. It was an eye-opener and an introduction to capitalism.

I was worried about flying but didn't share my thoughts with anyone, for fear of being judged an uneducated villager. I found my seat beside Kuol, a Sudanese fellow immigrating to Canada too. We tightened our seat belts as instructed and prepared for takeoff. My eyes remained wide open out of fear something would happen in the air and not wanting to lose the precious IOM sealed envelope. The food on the plane was unfamiliar but I ate it with gratitude since I was ravenous.

I would have lost my way without the aid of an IOM representative at the enormous and confusing London airport. We used subway trains (at that time I did not know what they were) and went through several airport checks. With looks of puzzlement or unease, many people observed fifty of us carrying the same IOM travel bags. Unlike the IOM in Kenya, we were fed at the airport during the six-hour stop over. Looking at my ticket, I was confused because it said it would take eight hours to fly from London to Toronto, yet we were leaving London at noon and arriving in Toronto at 3 p.m. the same day. I did not know about time zones and thought someone had made a mistake, but didn't ask for fear of being judged ignorant.

I had a window seat and took the opportunity to look about on that clear, sunny day as we departed from London, England. I could not believe we were soaring above the clouds! I prayed for travel mercies, knowing survival was zero if we crashed. Flight attendants offered various kinds of strange food and drink and I happily accepted, not knowing what it was. Before I knew it, we were told to tighten our belts and prepare for landing at Pearson International Airport in Toronto, Canada. Although sleep deprived, I was excited, not knowing I was about to experience temperatures like never before and a culture shock that no orientation session could adequately prepare me for.

# WHERE AM I?

Having lived many years in war-torn DR Congo and refugee camps, I dreamed of life in Canada, a land of plenty. On September 28, 2011 around 3 p.m., this dream became reality when my plane touched down at Toronto Pearson International Airport. I waited three hours to be processed at the port of entry designated for immigrants. After handing over my well-guarded sealed envelope and a five-minute interview, I was free to leave. Fortunately, a YMCA volunteer rescued me from my confusion, taking me to a small room where they were distributing resources to new immigrants. I was given plenty of brochures, books and newspapers introducing me to life in Canada. After collecting my luggage, I went to the passenger-receiving area to find my host family. Glancing around, I suddenly realized I was a visible minority, something I had never experienced before. Suddenly, my eyes caught a sign displaying, "Welcome to Canada Oliver!"

I was so excited to finally meet my host family who would become my adopted "Canadian family." I was greeted warmly by Bill and Marilyn and one of their four daughters, Julianna. Marilyn assumed I would be thirsty after the exhausting journey and brought me to a water fountain. I had never seen one before and began to use my right hand to cup the water, just as I had done from the river in Lusenda, DR Congo. She gently demonstrated how to drink from the fountain by bending my head and catching the water with my mouth, instead of my hand. This new experience instantly made me realize I was in an unfamiliar land and had a lot of learning ahead of me.

As we walked to the parking lot, it felt very chilly although people were walking around in T-shirts. According to my hosts, it was a balmy nine degrees Celsius that day, but I could not imagine surviving lower temperatures during a Canadian winter. As we left the airport and traveled to their home in Oshawa, I was amazed at the volume and speed of traffic on Highway 401. Within a few hours of landing, I realized I was unprepared for the fast pace and affluence of life in Canada.

Upon arrival at my Canadian family's home, I felt lost. The house had many rooms on three levels and I was told my bedroom was in the basement. I nodded but had no clue what "basement" meant. Their basement was a self-contained unit consisting of a kitchen, washroom, two bedrooms and large recreational room. I could not believe the space in a single family residence. I was overwhelmed with everything I had experienced that first day in Canada, including the hectic pace, skyscrapers, luxury vehicles, extensive highways, take-out food and subnormal temperatures.

I quickly encountered loneliness since there was no one who spoke my African languages. I could only converse with my host family using limited English, which became tiresome. At the same time, I was physically exhausted from jet-lag and emotionally drained, which intensified feelings of separation from family, friends and culture. Still, I remained determined to make Canada my new home.

During that first week in Canada, I obtained an interim federal health certificate, social insurance number and bank account with the help of Marilyn, who took a day off work. I felt my life was heading in a good direction and was blessed to no longer be considered a helpless refugee. Little did I know how disconcerting and stressful it would be to adjust and secure work in this land of plenty.

I staggered at the abundance of food and variety of choices the first time I went grocery shopping in Canada. When asked what I wanted, I simply responded "rice, beans, sweet potatoes and fish." Since birth, I had only known three kinds of rice but now I was faced with a wide variety, including white, brown, red, black, basmati, jasmine, wild, instant and much more. The whole experience gave me an overwhelming headache.

I began to discern what to buy in the grocery store with the help of Christine, a Registered Holistic Nutritionist who also attended the FreeWay. She volunteered to teach me how to shop for groceries, getting the most nutritious food for the best price. I was shocked to learn how prevalent junk food and soft drinks were. I had never read labels on food containers in Africa since we bought fresh produce and eggs from a local farmer. As we moved around the Canadian grocery store, Christine warned me to avoid foods that were poor nutritional choices, especially food and drink that was high in sugar, sodium and unhealthy fat. After a few weeks of shopping with her, I became an expert reading food labels and avoided processed food as much as possible. I felt blessed and thankful to have Christine's guidance, as she taught me how to maintain healthy eating habits despite the appeal of packaging, advertisements and convenience.

In my new Canadian home, I was expected to cook and clean for myself. This came as a disappointment since I fully expected my new Canadian mother to do the cooking and cleaning for the entire household, as was the norm back in Africa. However, she worked full-time outside the home and since I was an adult, I was expected to manage independently. In the first week I experienced my first migraine, triggered by new foods and sensory over-load. I asked for something to relieve my pain, not having access to the medicinal leaves from the bush back home. I soon learned that a small pill (Acetaminophen) could alleviate my symptoms.

I was shocked to realize how much Africa meant to me and how wrong my assumptions were about the "easy" life in Canada. So many emotions clouded my thoughts those first few weeks. Indeed, I was not worried about starvation or shootings but my mind was preoccupied with how to adjust in Canada. How could my dreams come true? I wondered how to get my educational credentials accepted. Several people had told me it was very difficult for immigrants to get their educational credentials approved in Canada. Although I was happy to be in Canada, at the same time I wondered, "Where am I?"

Through my culture shock, I discovered that settling in Canada was not simply a matter of adapting but also facing the challenge of maintaining lifelong beliefs and values while at the same time embracing innovative ways of living in a new country. I remained steadfast in my sense of purpose, moral framework and commitments which were greatly influenced by my culture of origin, spirituality and family. In just a few days in Canada, I felt my beliefs and values were put to the test and I needed to re-evaluate and re-affirm them.

My first church service in Canada was not what I expected. I missed the exuberant clapping, dancing and joyful shouts in African churches. Despite the noticeable difference in worship styles, I knew my sponsoring church of less than fifty attendees at the time, had a great love for people because they sponsored me and my friend John to come to Canada as refugees from war-torn DR Congo.

When Pastor Dale invited me to introduce myself, I quickly shared about my life during the war in DR Congo and how I felt God had used many people to orchestrate my coming to Canada: "It all started in Burundi with an American family named Bob and Laurie. The two introduced me to every American who visited Hope Africa University. In the summer of 2007, Professor Paul and Carol came to Hope to teach short-term and as usual, Laurie invited me to join them for a dinner. At the dinner table she told Paul and Carol how much she appreciated me and if they did anything for them, they should do it for Msenwa Oliver Mweneake. Over a year later, in September 2008, I could not believe reading an email from Professor Paul about the possibility of immigrating to Canada. Marilyn was willing to apply to Immigration Canada on my behalf and had asked the Free Methodist Church in Canada to be the "official" sponsor, through its small congregation in Oshawa — through you. Marilyn had agreed to help John immigrate to Canada (at the request of Professor Paul) but she felt strongly that another single male refugee should be included. Professor Paul recalled meeting me at the home of Bob and Laurie and that is how I came into the picture and became that second refugee."

I will never forget that first Sunday morning when I met the FreeWay congregation who had committed to support me in prayer, time and finances. At the end of the service people came to extend a warm welcome. I felt blessed to know how much everyone cared about me. I thanked everyone for supporting the idea of sponsoring me.

In the first two weeks in Canada, I spent many afternoons on the phone talking with friends and family back in Africa, using discount long distance telephone cards. I felt consoled any time I could speak Ebembe (my mother-tongue). After the phone call, I would get back to reading material for my last on-line course in the Master's program I had started in Kenya. My goal was to complete my studies in October and then focus the rest of my time on my thesis. As much as I loved studying, I was apprehensive that my education would not be recognized in Canada.

On Thanksgiving Day, my four Canadian sisters along with their husbands took me to a farm that grew corn and pumpkins. My parents had grown pumpkins in DR Congo but I was astonished to see people pay money for pumpkins they were not going to eat! I was also shocked when my Canadian sisters invited me to play hide and seek in the corn maze on the farm. The whole idea perplexed me. Why would people pay to play in a corn maze? I recalled many times in Lusenda when we had played in corn fields: I never got lost and never had to pay!

I quickly learned that Thanksgiving was a special celebration in Canada. I was happy to spend Thanksgiving with my Canadian family and enjoyed learning about this tradition. My new family was equally curious about my Bembe traditions. They asked me many questions and wanted to know about various celebrations in DR Congo. I was eager to share about my culture but my English was still inadequate.

I agreed to allow Marilyn to serve as my English teacher, correcting my pronunciation and teaching me new words, as well as new customs. I was like a little baby learning to walk, but excited to improve my English. I quickly learned not to raise my eyebrows as is the custom in Africa when indicating "yes" and I discovered how important direct eye contact was for Canadians. My Canadian family and church friends embraced me and spent time exposing me to new Canadian experiences. I recall my first hockey game, super bowl gathering, movie at the theatre, ice skating, buffet meal, dentist visit, subway ride and so much more.

I spent hours and hours learning about Canadian history from Bill. The two of us connected well and we explored the world through Google maps. I was amazed by his passion and knowledge of world history. Unlike many people I had spoken to in Canada, he knew all about the continent of Africa, understanding it was made up of fifty-four fully recognized sovereign states or countries. He also knew that Africa is the world's second-largest continent with over 1 billion people. Bill was very knowledgeable about DR Congo and its tumultuous history, as if he was Congolese himself. We would then jump to Kenyan, Tanzanian, South African, British, European and North American history. World history flowed from his mouth like water.

I recall the many times Bill and Marilyn would talk to me about life in Canada while sitting in their living room. Although I was bombarded with new experiences, I felt happy to live with them and learn many valuable lessons sooner rather than later. They were both passionate about social justice and eager to see me excel. They discussed finances, including the pros and cons of debt, enabling me to understand Canadian finances and ways to become financially independent. I was blessed to be in their house.

Marilyn's love for immigrants had already compelled them to host several immigrants before John and I came to live with them.

My Canadian family tried hard to initiate me in all aspects of Canadian life. One Sunday afternoon, they suggested I take their dog for a walk. They convinced me to do so by claiming (as a joke, although I didn't realize) it would prove I was becoming Canadian. This was a different way of thinking for me — I had never seen a dog being walked by its owner in Africa and yet here in Canada, it was a common occurrence. I was flabbergasted to hear about the amount of money spent in North America on pets, for food, grooming, veterinary care, toys, accessories and even overnight accommodation when people went on vacation. I was determined to embrace this new culture as long as it did not contradict my own values and beliefs, which included a sense of responsible stewardship.

I eagerly joined Bill and Marilyn in picking up my friend John from Toronto Pearson International Airport in October 2011. John and I knew each other very well since we both had been in Nyarugusu refugee camp and both studied at Hope Africa University in Burundi. We both came from Fizi and had similar life experiences. While studying at Hope Africa University, we were part of Neno La Uzima — the university choir — and also members of the Congolese Association. The basement was not as lonely once John arrived. We would joke and laugh in Ebembe, pointing out cultural differences.

John's coming made it easier for both of us since we

could support each other and I was happy to have someone to converse with in Ebembe. I realized that was why Marilyn advocated for two refugees.

The two of us went on exploration walks around Oshawa. We would joke at ourselves as we looked around and realized we were a visible minority. Nevertheless, we were proud to be in a safe and accepting country. Just like in DR Congo, we would innocently hold hands as we walked the streets of Oshawa. Embedded in our African culture is the holding of hands while walking with a friend: it is a visible sign of close friendship and understanding. We assumed the same in Canada but later learned that our hand holding could be misinterpreted, which explained why people stared at us and gave unusual glances.

Before long it was Christmas in Canada, which triggered shock over the differences in cultural celebrations. In Africa, the focus of Christmas was around church attendance. Beginning as early as October, various churches would start making contributions of food and money towards the upcoming Christmas gathering. More than a thousand people from different villages and local churches would come to my village, Lusenda, or another selected village to celebrate Christmas. The events would often start on Thursday afternoon and end on Sunday afternoon. Different speakers would be invited to talk about the meaning and essence of Christmas and other related subjects. Over ten choirs would present their self-composed music each day. It was a time of baptism, committing lives to Christ, laughter, celebration and building long-lasting relationships.

During my first Christmas in Canada in 2011, the focus appeared to be on gift-giving and spending time with family. John and I could not believe that church attendance was limited to a few services, instead of several days. John and I walked to the Oshawa Shopping Centre the week before Christmas and found it flooded with a multitude of shoppers. I supposed there must be a looming strike so people had to make purchases before the stores closed. I later learned that people were shopping because it was Christmas time.

Coming from a small village, I was disturbed to observe the commercialization of Christmas. TV commercials were constantly sending a message to buy out of want, not need. This contradicted my understanding of stewardship. I did not want to buy gifts for people who were not impoverished, knowing others on the other side of the world were in desperate need. However, I also didn't want to estrange myself from my new culture. The gifts I received were incomparable to anything I had ever received in my life span. I was grateful to see how people were willing to give gifts during Christmas but wondered if much of the gift-giving came out of cultural expectation.

After Christmas, I continued looking for work and submitted over one hundred resumes, without a response. My friend John, who arrived in Canada three weeks after me, had secured his first job at "A & W." I knew I did not have Canadian experience and training but I was confident I had transferable skills and knowledge, given my undergraduate and Master's degree. I desperately sought employment, believing there was an entry level position in my field of Social Work. I would soon discover another dimension of the immigrant experience as I faced discouragement and stress with my first job in Canada.

## 22

# WHY AM I HERE?

Looking for a job became my full-time job as I applied to numerous postings, day after day. When I became disheartened, Marilyn recommended I go to the YMCA to connect with an employment counsellor while affirming, "I know you are qualified for more than a minimum wage job." I did not know anything about "minimum wage" until she explained it to me. As she searched in the evenings for appropriate entry level positions, she felt confident a job in community services would open up, allowing me to gain "Canadian" experience in the social work field. This inspired hope, despite hearing over and over from potential employers, "You seem to be a nice fit but you do not have Canadian experience."

I decided to volunteer at a nearby school, making use of every opportunity to obtain "experience" while trying to gain entrance into the Canadian job market. I learned about the Canadian educational system as I assisted in various classrooms. I felt useful and appreciated, since I was able to use my French, Swahili and other African languages to help the parents of students overcome their language barrier. I also started to volunteer at the Community Development Council in Durham. As a volunteer I was encouraged by affirmations that I had transferable skills to flourish in a job. At the same time, the agony of spending countless hours searching for gainful employment weighed me down. I wondered, "Why am I here?"

The advice to connect with the YMCA was valuable and I had several inspiring meetings with Terry-Ann, an employment counsellor. I shared my educational background and employment history and together we identified goals and steps to reach them. In our second meeting, Terry-Ann assisted me in drafting an attractive and job-focused resume. Through her support, the YMCA also paid for a "First Aid and CPR" course as well as other training, enhancing my skills for employment in my field of interest.

Waiting for the bus in Oshawa, Ontario became unbearable during January of 2012 since the bitter cold chilled me to the bone, despite several layers of clothes. On one such day, I met Edwin. We soon became engrossed in conversation as he shared how his parents immigrated to Canada from Tanzania before he was born. He alluded to some of the struggles his parents went through as new immigrants to Canada and I shared mine. Edwin was excited to learn that I spoke Swahili and insisted I meet his parents someday, since they spoke it too. Learning of my desperate search for employment, Edwin suggested Optima Communications International but warned, "It's a tough job, but better than nothing."

As soon as I arrived home, I went to the internet and discovered several openings for the position of Sales Representative (telemarketer) at Optima Communications International. I had attended enough job search workshops to know that I needed to apply immediately or I would miss out. I received my first response to a job application when Optima Communications International invited me to an interview. Although I had no previous experience with telemarketing, I was confident that I had transferable skills and assumed my languages would be an asset.

I arrived early for the interview, since cultural orientation classes in Kenya had emphasized the need to be "on time" in the Canadian culture. Tardiness would not be tolerated and I took the advice seriously. After completing an on-line test, I was ushered into another room for a verbal exchange with the hiring manager. I was bombarded with questions about telemarketing and insurance sales. I felt confident about the interview. The manager called me the following day to offer me the job and set my start date for Monday, January 31, 2012 with a week-long orientation. I was entering uncharted territory but thrilled to get my first paying job in Canada and happy when I was told I would receive a little more compensation for being bilingual (able to speak English and French). At the same time, I felt badly that I would not be available in the day time to continue volunteering.

My first few days in the telemarketing field comprised of an introduction to Optima's organizational structure and mission, with an overview of core businesses and the merits of selling insurance. On the third day, all fifteen new hires were told to start making telephone sales. At the end of the shift, a few people on my team had made sales, but I was unsuccessful. I had never done telemarketing and was terrified about selling accidental death insurance since talking about death was taboo in my culture. However, I persevered out of desperation for Canadian work experience.

At the end of the third day, I asked myself if I should continue in telemarketing. When I arrived home, I shared my distress about the job. Marilyn smiled and said, "That's a tough job, Oliver, but you are only there for a short time. Remember my motto — short term pain for long term gain." Her words encouraged me but I could not think about anything else that evening. It was humbling to find myself in such an uncomfortable situation. I never dreamed I could hate a job as much as I hated this one. A myriad of thoughts and emotions bombarded me the whole night: new country, new job, new language, new culture…everything was new.

I wrestled with thoughts of quitting but then voices of family members came to mind: "fight until your last breath — life on earth will never be easy but you were born to be resilient." I decided to banish all the negative thoughts that were paralyzing me. I took a few minutes to meditate and pray in preparation for the day.

At work I had to take a test involving multiple choice questions as well as a practical section dealing with accidental death insurance. I breezed through the written section but was apprehensive about the evaluator listening to my foreign accent as I discussed accidental death insurance. Being so new to Canada, I was relieved to know I passed, since several did not. I still had to complete a test in French since my employer wanted to verify I was truly bilingual. After being connected to their Toronto office, I was tested and passed with flying colours, since French is like my first language. The bilingual certification meant I would be paid an extra two dollars per hour.

My work days were spent trying to sell accidental death insurance over the phone. I felt like a failure, unable to score one sale in days. More than five people who started with me had already quit, unable to take it. I felt trapped without an alternative. It was distasteful, to say the least, listening to people scream and curse at you and then hang up. Adjusting to life in Canada was one thing, but telemarketing was repugnant. I knew it wasn't personal but it was hurtful to hear a barrage of negative comments, phone call after phone call. I pondered after my first week of employment, "Why I am here?"

The second week was even worse. The pressure to make sales escalated. The team leader would shout, "Get on the board, Oliver! I have not seen your name on the board since you started!" I cringed and wanted to hide. Over fifty people worked each shift, packed into tiny cubicles, chattering vigorously to customers through their head phones. Everyone was trying to make a sale. I was shocked at the number of sales some people could make and yet I could not get one.

I knew I was not born for telemarketing but equated quitting with failure. Each shift at Optima brought its own emotions, ranging from confusion to desperation, helplessness and a sense of failure. I battled with myself day after day as I sat in my cubicle trying to sell a product I would never buy myself. My values were put to the test, but I needed the Canadian experience. I longed to see the end of each shift. Thankfully, connections formed with some of my coworkers and these friendships carried me through the stressful days. Debra, a middle-aged Caribbean lady, became a supportive colleague and we spent our breaks reminding each other that God's grace was sufficient in the midst of our difficulties. I persisted through my first month, telling myself that my dream job was yet to come.

Most Canadians were polite outside of the telemarketing world but I quickly learned they disliked telemarketers. While many opted to swear at me, I was fascinated when a few took the opportunity to encourage me. One day, I was inspired and touched by one customer. He listened politely as I recited my script and then responded in a gentle manner, "I can't imagine how tough your job must be, reminding people they will someday die in order to sell them your product. But I want you to know that I love you and wish the best for you. Even more so, the Creator loves you and we can find hope for this life and the next through Him." Tears of joy streamed down my face as I listened to his kind words; words that meant so much more to me than selling a product ever could. Once again, a complete stranger had invested in me — this time with verbal encouragement.

I anticipated getting fired, after the Optima team leader told my group that he would have to let some of us go due to low sales. That exhausting shift in March 2012 was again unproductive and I thought he was looking directly at me when the warning was issued. I felt embarrassed but soon learned I was not the only one. I knew many of us were trying hard but no one seemed to acknowledge our efforts. By now, only four people remained out of the fifteen that I had started with. The turnover was extremely high and I understood why. It wasn't worth the stress and verbal abuse.

The job became more unbearable each day but I resolved to never miss a single day of work until I had secured another job. I endured so I could send support to my parents in the refugee camp. During times of questioning, I found solace in trusting that my Maker held my life in his hands and was aware of my every thought and tear. I believed my heavenly Father would never leave me, no matter where I was.

# FUTURE GAIN

Some people had admonished me that my African degree was worthless in Canada. Remembering how God had used various people to fund my education, I had to believe it was not in vain. While enduring the stressful telemarketing job, the FreeWay Free Methodist church graciously paid the fee to have my Social Work degree evaluated by the Canadian Association of Social Workers (CASW). My cousin Joseph, still on campus at Hope Africa University in Burundi, expedited the mailing of my official transcripts directly to the CASW.

My Canadian family and I held many discussions regarding education and career options. Out of these discussions, I learned about a new on-line Master's of Social Work program through the University of Waterloo, starting in the summer of 2012. I paid the on-line fee to register, using Marilyn's credit card since I didn't have one yet. The next few weeks were busy as I completed my thesis for my Master's in Leadership and Business from Kenya, while continuing my stressful job and at the same time searching for another. Though I was busy from morning to night, I was happy and confident that my life was heading in the right direction.

As days went by, I eagerly awaited the results of my undergraduate degree evaluation as well as the outcome of my application to the University of Waterloo. Towards the end of February, Marilyn forwarded a job posting for a community service worker at Cornerstone Community Association, a men's hostel in Oshawa. I quickly applied for the part-time job and two weeks later was called for an interview. By then I had attended several interviews but this was the first in my field and I wanted the job badly. I arrived twenty minutes early, allowing time to scan the lobby, making as many observations as possible. I noted mostly white men, prompting the question, *Will they hire a newly landed black immigrant in a place where the majority are white?*

The interview lasted over one hour and included various case scenarios. To this day I remember laughing with Rob, the manager, over the answers I gave. He queried, "Say a client was in front of you needing help and at the same time, the police call you but before you can say a word to the police, someone tells you that another client is on the floor upstairs and they think he might be dying. What would you do and why?" I smiled as I began my answer, "I would first inform the client in front of me as well as the police that I needed to respond to an emergency because my top priority would be the client upstairs — from a business perspective, clients are what keep us in business. If we run out of clients, we are out of business." Rob stared at me for a minute in apparent shock and then burst out laughing as he exclaimed, "In all my years of interviewing, I have never heard anyone respond from a business perspective!" I laughed too, relieved that my potential manager seemed to like my response.

It was my turn to ask a few questions, wanting to learn about the challenges I would face. I appreciated Rob's honest responses, especially when he confirmed my observation that the shelter was dominated by white clients and staff. "I am not sure how some clients will react to a black, male staff member, especially someone new to the country with an accent but I feel like you have the courage and skills to turn challenges into opportunities," he affirmed.

Hope was renewed when I was offered a part-time job at Cornerstone Community Association. Orientation involved learning about regulations, the computer system and paperwork, which was fascinating. It was a new experience and I was enthusiastic to excel. Unfortunately, after completing orientation, I was dismissed home on my first shift because Corrections Canada had not received my police check results.

Since I was new to the country, it took longer to get a federal police check done. Fortunately, I had decided to continue part-time work with Optima until I was sure of my financial stability with the position at Cornerstone Community Association. While waiting for the police check results, I received mail from the Canadian Association of Social Workers. The letter indicated my undergraduate Social Work degree was equivalent to a Bachelor of Social Work (BSW) in Canada. I was overjoyed to think that now my dreams could come true.

A month later the police check cleared and I was able to resume work at Cornerstone Community Association. The team embraced me but I needed to prove myself as a newcomer to Canada, not yet fluent in English. I prided myself in people skills and cultural competencies. I was curious and open-minded, willing to listen and understand diverse worldviews.

After the first week on the job, I had built excellent rapport with clients and colleagues. Several told me that they appreciated my big smile, genuineness, authenticity and helpfulness. Many of the homeless men nicknamed me "Smiley." I laughed with them and listened to their stories. I often joked with the men, including a gruff, former convict. My manager was alarmed, thinking the ex-convict would knock my lights out, but he was accepting and we bantered back and forth. I was glad the clients felt comfortable confiding in me. The shelter reminded me of when I was homeless, sleeping under trees and begging for survival. I connected with the men and tried to inspire hope and possibilities.

I received an offer of admission from the University of Waterloo after they confirmed I had taken English based Master's program in Kenya. We began with a one-week intensive course at the University of Waterloo in August

2012. Over thirty students were registered in the program, the majority women. I found this interesting since in Burundi, the majority of my classmates were men. I successfully completed the initial one-week intensive course and was well-positioned to complete the rest, since it was mostly on-line. I used my on-line skills to assist other students in navigating the computer-based program, having acquired these skills while studying in Kenya. Again, I reminded myself that my education in Africa was not in vain.

With optimistic thoughts about the future, a desire for a life-partner stirred within my soul. While harbouring feelings of apprehension and mistrust from the past relationship break up, Pastor Dale from the Freeway church encouraged me to keep an open heart and mind as I continued to trust God for leading. I valued his mentorship and our weekly meetings supported my transition to Canadian life.

Who could imagine a ninety-two year old man acting as a matchmaker, yet it was Grandpa James who introduced me to Miriam at Wesley Acres Campground. We were introduced in September 2012 and I immediately felt my search for a girlfriend had come to an end, although at first Miriam showed no romantic interests. I could not stop looking at this beautiful, blue-eyed lady with an attractive smile, delightful laugh and inner peace that compelled me to want to know her.

Miriam shared her passion for social justice and desire to help others, talking about experiences in Colombia, working to empower displaced communities affected by the fifty-year armed conflict. By the end of the first day, I knew the two of us had similar passions. We ended our time together by eagerly exchanging contact information, planning to keep in touch. The following weeks were filled with hour-long phone conversations as we shared about our families, our hopes and our life goals.

Two months later, I went to visit Miriam in Waterloo. I was wholeheartedly accepted by her Grandma, where Miriam was staying. Our dating relationship began formally that weekend and as we parted, we shared excitement about our new relationship. The opportunity to meet Miriam's family came in December 2012 when I attended the wedding of Victoria (my Canadian family's youngest daughter) in Napanee, Ontario.

My anxiety over meeting Miriam's family dissipated as they welcomed me — a black man from war-torn Congo. I felt at home as everyone showed genuine interest in my life and culture. Miriam and I spent time cooking together, laughing and working as a team. Those joyful few days passed quickly. I then traveled to the United States to visit Professor Paul in Rochester and my cousin Ndanga in Buffalo. Miriam became the news of the month. I could not wait to inform my parents and friends in Africa about my budding relationship.

It was thrilling to speak in my mother-tongue with my cousin and his family. During the visit with my cousin Ndanga in Buffalo, we spent the evening talking and singing Ebembe songs. We had not seen each other since he left Kenya in 2010. Ndanga's family was excited to talk over Skype with the special girl who might one day become a member of our family. During that visit, I called my parents in Africa to let them know about my relationship with Miriam. I was amazed at how supportive everyone was, offering their prayers and support for our relationship. I returned to Oshawa to continue work at Cornerstone Community Association, my heart filled with hope. My life was taking a new direction, with dreams and aspirations for a stable life and that special someone to share the journey with.

## 24

# HOPE RESTORED

As I write this chapter, I recall many times I felt discouraged and dejected. Like many immigrants, I thought life would be easy from the moment I landed in Canada. I wondered why I had adverted death so many times. I reminded myself of the determination and resilience that had sustained me when I was uprooted from my home in DR Congo, forced to subsist in a refugee camp and labelled a worthless refugee in Kenya. None of these transitions were easy. Many times I had reached the point of hopelessness and helplessness. The only thing that had been certain in my life was uncertainty. I remembered my Grandpa's words: "You cannot give up your dream. You have to push through the highs and lows of life. You must have faith and persevere to find your way." Through it all, I held fast to the belief that everything was for a purpose and that the constant turmoil would come to an end.

Through the ups and downs of life, my parents had taught me that work was not a punishment but something I should pursue and be proud of. I focused on success stories about immigrants who had excelled in their respective fields, although few. I was frustrated to not reach my income potential, yet remained committed to my current job in order to provide for myself and family across the world. I wanted to utilize my education and knowledge to the maximum, instead of feeling inadequate in a complex system.

I took every opportunity to acquire new information and attended a workshop on credit and borrowing in Canada. The benefits and dangers of having a credit card were reinforced. I had taken a student loan to pay the remaining tuition for my Master's in Social Work, yet remained uneasy about debt because it was ingrained in me to avoid it. I felt frustrated about the lack of money to support my family in the way I wanted but I also didn't want to accumulate debt that would become a life-long burden. Strong internal voices upheld the conviction, "Oliver, you were born for a great purpose. Strive to become a better you. Pain is only short term."

As I continued to work through the painful transition to life in Canada, I received a message from home that stirred panic within. News came that my Mother was in the hospital, near death with malaria. I knew she would not receive the best of care in the camp and that the mortality rate was high there. I was angry there was little medical aid for people in the camp and more died of malaria than any other disease. My parents, siblings and friends routinely contracted malaria. I was afraid that my Mother's weakened immune system from poor nutrition and unsanitary living conditions would destroy her ability to fight yet another bout. I felt inadequate, unable to do anything but pray.

While death was hovering over my Mother, I tried to reflect on evidence of divine intervention in my past. I felt indebted to my church (FreeWay Free Methodist Church), the Whitby YMCA, Cornerstone Community Association, the Durham Francophone Settlement Program and many individuals all over the world. Still, I struggled to concentrate at work, believing my Mother was dying in Nyarugusu refugee camp with very little treatment options. The next few days were very emotional as I waited for updates on her status. As I biked home from work around midnight, I was so preoccupied about my Mother's infirmity that I was almost hit by a car.

"It is a miracle you are still with us."

Good news came twice the next week. I was overjoyed to learn that my Mother, although very weak, was well enough to be discharged from the hospital and I was elated when requested to attend an interview for a position at the Hincks-Dellcrest Centre. They were seeking a bilingual (French and English) person with a Master's in Social Work. The job would be an amazing opportunity for me to use my French and possibly other African languages, especially since the centre was located in downtown Toronto, but I wondered if I would be disqualified since I was still studying to obtain my Master's degree.

I wanted it all and I wanted it now! I expected a good job,

with good pay in this land of promise. From my perspective, it was a slow process but Marilyn often reminded me that I was being "fast tracked" as she watched in amazement at how quickly things were happening in my favour. She reminded me how I had received my first job within four months of landing, quickly obtained my education credentials, secured another job in the social service field and enrolled in the Master's of Social Work at the University of Waterloo. I now had an upcoming interview in February 2013 for a senior Social Worker position and I had a Canadian girlfriend. Indeed, many blessings surrounded my dissapointments.

I prepared for the upcoming interview by reading about the agency, a practice that I learned in Canada. I arrived for the interview in plenty of time, thankful that Dave from my church had previously assisted me in navigating the Greater Toronto Area (GTA) transit system. The two interviewers tested my understanding of social work practices as well as my command of French and English. I was also asked to list key qualities that would make me an asset for any employer: strong work ethic, great sense of humour, honest, flexible, adaptable and quick to learn. I left the interview doubtful I would get the job because I had not completed my Master's in Social Work, a key requirement for the position.

At home, numerous messages arrived from around the world, expressing love and encouragement regarding the potential job. This lifted my spirits to immeasurable heights. Not long after, tears of joy streamed down my face when Ellen from the Hincks-Dellcrest Centre confirmed I was the successful candidate. I was elated since others had said it takes years before an immigrant can get a job in their field. Marilyn believed I was meant to immigrate to Canada where my fluency in French gave me a competitive edge. I was jubilant that my life was heading in the right direction. It was obvious God had provided and guided to this point.

The Hincks-Dellcrest Centre consisted of an amazing interdisciplinary team, passionate about making a positive impact in lives. My supervisor and all the staff supported me as I settled into the position. One of the most valuable learning opportunities came through live supervision: while I provided therapy to a family, my supervisor Ellen sat behind a one-way mirror and communicated with me through an earpiece. I was encouraged by her feedback as I learned to integrate new therapy approaches into my practice.

The value of community was in my life blood and I had that in Oshawa, through my Canadian family and church connections. Regrettably, I had to make the move to Toronto since the long commute from Oshawa was physically and emotionally draining. I did not know anyone in my new neighbourhood and the big city did not appear friendly. I was perplexed because I was taught we were made for connections. Growing up with seven sisters in a large extended family within a village, we were all connected. In Toronto, I felt isolated and overwhelmed with loneliness.

Around the same time, I proposed to my girlfriend, Miriam. Family and friends all over the world celebrated our engagement. I looked forward to having my beloved join me in Toronto after our wedding in four months. In the meantime, I busied myself with the new job and studied diligently to complete my Master's in Social Work.

Miriam and I were joyfully wed on November 30, 2013 at Kingston West Free Methodist Church in Kingston, Ontario, with Pastor Dale from my home church as the officiant. More than one hundred people joined us to celebrate, including my cousins Lucy and Furaha (who had immigrated to Canada and were living in British Columbia), my cousin Ndanga from Buffalo and a nephew from Quebec. Bill and Marilyn offered to stand in for my parents. I felt blessed that their whole family had adopted me.

We gathered at Rideau Acres Resort for the reception where the "white corn flour" (snow) blanketed the ground. As a child, I had never imagined having a white wedding because snow was unheard of in DR Congo. Although the wedding was small, I knew my parents in Nyarugusu refugee camp were also celebrating with over two hundred guests gathered to sing, dance, pray and eat.

At the reception hall, I marveled at the colourful decorations my wife and her sister and friends had provided for our wedding. We took wedding pictures outside a frozen fountain — a new experience for this Congo boy who was still adapting to the cold. We revelled in the moments with each other and everyone around us. The speeches of family and friends brought me to tears as I reflected on the countless miracles that had brought me safely to this day.

Since the beginning of our relationship, we spent hours in the kitchen cooking and joking about many things, including our nicknames "blackee" and "whitee." I did not grow up with recipe books while Miriam did, so we often created new recipes from scratch, using both our diverse upbringings and creativity. As a new unit, we came to appreciate the uniqueness and diversity of our cultures. It has been fascinating to discover how much of our life is socially constructed — from food to relationships, everyday conversations, finances, family and much more.

Despite the differences in race, colour and culture, we saw each other's values and passions as the binding force that brought us together to serve the Creator, others and each other. Marriage not only brought excitement but also a desire to pursue dreams that had once seemed unattainable. Miriam and I rejuvenated each other's passion for social justice and peace as we encouraged each other to seek opportunities every day to serve and empower those around us and beyond.

The first months of our marriage flew by as we adjusted to life together. We had agreed to defer our honeymoon until I could get time off work. Then, we would take a trip to Tanzania, including a visit to Nyarugusu refugee camp, so Miriam could meet her in-laws. This was Miriam's first visit to the continent of Africa and it would be the first time for me to return since immigrating to Canada in 2011.

# BITTERSWEET

As we boarded the plane, survivor's guilt weighed heavily on me. It was April 2014 and my new bride and I were heading to Africa for our honeymoon and to visit my parents and sisters in Nyarugusu refugee camp. My mind could not stop asking, "Why me?" I knew how difficult life was in the camp due to poor sanitation, inadequate food and shelter, along with overwhelming helplessness and despair.

After a week of rest and relaxation in the capital of Tanzania, we boarded a flight to the town of Kigoma, located on the far west side of Tanzania near Lake Tanganyika. I was anxious about seeing Kigoma again, the place where I had been labelled a refugee for the first time. Our landing in Kigoma triggered traumatic memories about the war on the other side of Lake Tanganyika and yet, I was also excited to see family and friends.

Lake Tanganyika brought back so many memories. It

connected me to the land of my ancestors and reminded me of dreadful butchery, rape, torture and the loss of innocent friends and family. An unusual mix of sorrow and expectation filled my heart as I stared across the lake to my home district of Fizi. This was the place where I had felt all my hopes and dreams were crushed. This time, however, I was a different person — a person who, through the support of many, had overcome what seemed to be insurmountable.

An hour later, we found ourselves packed into an overcrowded mini-bus heading to Nyarugusu refugee camp. The first twenty minutes of smooth travel ended abruptly as the vehicle's wheels hit the red dirt road. Dust swirled around us for the remaining four-hour journey, finding its way into our ears, eyes, clothes, and anywhere else it could sneak in. When we arrived, we did not look white or black but had become a new race: bright red. We finally arrived at the village of Makere where my parents and church members were eagerly waiting. Tears of joy flowed down my face as I was reunited with my parents and sisters for the first time in several years. I joyfully introduced my family to my beautiful bride.

My heart broke as I learned about the current conditions in the camp. It was substandard and more impoverished than when I had last visited seven years prior. Basic health care and shelter was inadequate. Unsanitary latrines contributed to disease. Violence against girls was on the increase. Refugees were still restricted from leaving the camp and thereby denied employment, forcing sole reliance on humanitarian assistance. Schools and health care facilities were literally crumbling. I cried out in anguish, "Will this suffering ever end?"

My whole family was still on the same plot as nineteen years ago — D1, cluster 9, plot 4. I cried as I entered the grass-roofed house that I had slept in before. I remembered how my family and many others had hoped to return to their homes in DR Congo, but now, nearly twenty years later, they were still stuck here, going nowhere. Nothing had changed for the better.

With my limited resources, I was thrilled to be able to finance a two hundred person seminar to encourage leadership within the camp. As I led the seminar, I realized there was little I could change during my brief visit. While there, many emphasized the need for scholarships so high school graduates could pursue university studies. "We do not know if we will leave the camp alive but we want our children to have opportunities and hope for the future," implored parents.

My mind reflected on the sacrifices of various people who had supported my studies and I knew I had to "pay it forward." I knew that upon return to Canada I had to write my story, hoping it would remind the world that sixty-eight thousand of my fellow Congolese were barely surviving in Nyarugusu refugee camp. I committed to become a change agent for those languishing in the camp.

The journey back to Nyarugusu refugee camp was a time of remorse, reflection and resolution. I could not dispel the sadness it evoked from flashbacks of the war in DR Congo, horrendous times in the refugee camp and feelings of despair and hopelessness. At the same time, a dream was birthed. Suffering could end with the help of others. I recognized I was "still with us" because many had helped me along the way, including Almighty God. It was my turn to help others.

Back in Toronto, I reflected on the trip and envisioned possibilities to be a positive change agent. My wife and I started a blog where we could share about Nyarugusu refugee camp and what is happening in DR Congo. At the same time we initiated the process to establish "The Msenwa Foundation" and register it as a charity in Canada, with a focus on supporting widows and orphans and providing other supports to Congolese in DR Congo and elsewhere, especially those in exile. With the help of friends, family and church members, we also raised funds to send several Nyarugusu high school graduates to university in Burundi.

After graduating from the University of Waterloo with a Master's in Social Work, I could no longer stifle my dream to equip fellow Africans to address the challenges that our continent is facing. Social work is still new in many African countries, Burundi in particular, making it hard to secure qualified professors. With the experience and skills acquired in my everyday practice at the Hincks-Dellcrest Centre in providing psychotherapy to children and families, I knew it was time to give back to the university where I received my undergraduate degree in Social Work.

Through personal savings and friends, I raised enough funds to cover a volunteer teaching trip to Hope Africa University in March 2015. The joy of returning to equip my fellow Africans surpassed all other emotions and jet-lag. I felt so many positive emotions as I arrived at Hope Africa University, the place that I had called home for four years. Seeing the dormitory and touching its walls revived so many memories, including endless hours studying by candlelight. I recalled chapel services and interpreting for others as well as the positive connections made with many from diverse cultures. I remembered being expelled due to lack of finances but later being given the chance to study through an anonymous sponsor from the United States.

Hope Africa University was a place of great struggle and desperation, yet it was also the place where, through the love of Bob and Laurie Hughes, the connection to immigrate to Canada was made. I was joyful for the opportunity to give back by teaching an intensive course on "Social Problems Affecting Youth in Africa." The course challenged many to consider alternative ways to support youth in post-conflict societies. As the course went on, I came to realize how much one must be empowered in order to empower others. Just like when I had returned to Nyarugusu refugee camp, I was no longer the same Oliver who was merely surviving. I was empowered because others had invested in me and as a result, my life changed in a dramatic way.

Talking with students and staff, I was heartbroken to hear that most of my countrymen cannot attain a university education due to lack of finances. From my own personal experience, I knew that education was the catalyst for change, a means to self-actualization and fulfillment. Education takes people to new heights, providing a sense of belonging and transforming them into a global citizen. I returned to Canada with a renewed passion to enable others to gain higher education, believing this is fundamental to empowering individuals, communities and nations in Africa.

As I write this book, I remember the many times I was hungry or had witnessed the murder of a beloved friend or relative as well as the desperation of life in the refugee camp, yet I understand that suffering is a shared experience for every human being. I remind myself that my life is not determined by circumstances but rather by the choices and responses I make. I have learned to be thankful for all the bad and good in life because that has made me who I am today. Throughout the journey, I have learned to appreciate the power that is available to every human being through connections with others, nature and the Creator.

Although I cursed struggles in the moment and would never wish them on anyone, my life was shaped because of them, especially how I perceive situations and people. I now see opportunities to inspire hope, build resilience and move beyond circumstances. I am where I am today because of those struggles and the many people who believed and invested in me. I have never known some of these people personally but I am thankful for their sacrifices.

As I look back, I can audaciously say if it were not for family, friends and those who invested in me, I would not be where I am today! I recognized at an early stage in my journey that human beings were made for relationship and that through this, we can survive the turmoil of life. However, it took me a long time to learn that anyone can make an impact in another's life. For quite a while, I considered the people who invested in me as super human beings with excess resources. However, I later discovered that most of these people had their own challenges and limitations, yet were determined to inspire hope in others by investing in them — whether financially, emotionally, spiritually or physically.

# FORSAKEN?

I remain overwhelmingly disturbed over current news about DR Congo with its unending reports of mass murder, systemic rape and ongoing atrocities of war. This has continued since the outbreak of fighting in 1996 when I was fifteen years old. More than eight million Congolese have died in DR Congo since then. My beautiful country has been labelled the "rape capital of the world" as women are systematically targeted and attacked on an unprecedented scale.

Reports focus on fighting in my former provinces of South Kivu and North Kivu in eastern DR Congo, near the Rwanda border. Human rights violations continue on an unparalleled scale. The murder of innocent Congolese is overlooked daily as their land, rich in natural resources like gold, copper, diamonds and coltan (a mineral used in cell phones) is exploited.

Currently the entire system and infrastructure is in shambles, including education and healthcare. Despite the country's rich natural resources, with untapped deposits of raw minerals estimated to be worth in excess of twenty-four trillion US dollars, Congolese are classified among the poorest in the world, having the second lowest Gross Domestic Product (GDP) per capita globally. More than two and a half million earn less than $1 US per day.

Every time I talk with friends and families back home, I am heartbroken by the atrocities and struggles my people are forced to endure daily. Those who are not subjected to violence must contend with poverty, famine and disease. Infant and child mortality rates (forty-seven percent of the deaths) are extremely high as a result of famine and malnutrition, exacerbated by war. One million children are orphaned as a direct or indirect result of war. Some sources indicate that forty-five thousand people continue to die in DR Congo each month. It is reported that over three million people have been displaced within DR Congo and over two million have become refugees in the neighbouring countries of Burundi, Rwanda, Tanzania and Uganda.

Despite modern progress world-wide, little has improved in my country since the 1980s when I was born. The national maternal mortality rate is one of the highest in the world. The UN reports there are approximately two thousand doctors for a population of fifty million in DR Congo with about forty-five percent in Kinshasa, leaving minimal medical assistance elsewhere. The prospects of raising Congolese physicians is low since displaced children have no school to attend and often are forced to become child soldiers, some under twelve years of age.

While the killing and rape of innocent Congolese continue inside the country, in Nyarugusu refugee camp where my family and friends live to this day, fear and uncertainty has increased ten-fold since April 2015 due to an influx of Burundian refugees. This has forced the end of education in the camp because schools were closed to provide shelter for the new arrivals.

The population of Nyarugusu refugee camp has now tripled and numbers continue to increase daily. Established in 1996, Nyarugusu refugee camp is one of the world's oldest camps and has been home to sixty-eight thousand Congolese. The UNHCR has made drastic cuts to all basic rations in recent years. With the addition of over one hundred and fifty thousand Burundian refugees, the camp's medical, educational and sanitation structures are collapsing. The death toll from diseases like cholera and malaria are on the rise.

Is there hope for the children of DR Congo? My Mother's words keep coming back to mind as I write these pages, "It is a miracle you are still with us." I am convinced I survived the horrors of war so I could be a voice to advocate for those left behind. I have written "Still With Us" to raise awareness of the plight of the Congolese in Nyarugusu refugee camp and DR Congo. Proceeds from this book are dedicated to bring hope in the midst of despair — to empower the Congolese through education and other supports.

I was given the opportunity to attend university and from this experience, I clearly see the transformative power it can have. Education is one of the main ways to eradicate poverty for an individual and country. The UN states that "education is the single best investment in prosperous, healthy and equitable societies." No country has ever achieved rapid and continuous economic growth without at least a forty-percent literacy rate. Children who complete primary education are more likely to end the cycle of poverty in their generation. Education increases confidence and self-sufficiency.

Having studied and lived in unbearable conditions, I found strength through education, the single most important driver of economic empowerment. As the war continues to ravage villages and cities in DR Congo, thousands of women become widowed, forcing them into deplorable situations. Education and skills are critical tools to economically empower them through sustainable projects.

My dream is that one day DR Congo will be restored to peace — where once again children are safe to play and resources will be used to benefit the Congolese, resulting in improved nutrition, health and education. I dream of the day DR Congo is free from exploitation.

To this day I reflect on the countless times I was without medical care, food, shoes, shelter, family and stability, but I hold no bitterness from these experiences. I now long to help victims regain hope, just as others restored mine. I know there is hope for anyone going through horrific times, if we look at suffering and pain as part of the shared human experience and take the opportunity to help each other through it. I cannot stop thanking the many people who believed and invested in me over the years and the only way I can repay them is by giving my life in service to others. "The Msenwa Foundation" was established to restore hope and a positive future for the Congolese people and to provide an affirmative response to the cries of the Congolese when they ask, "Is anyone still with us?"

To learn how you can help and partner in the restoration of hope, visit:

www.msenwafoundation.com

## About the Author

Msenwa Oliver Mweneake was born and happily lived most of his childhood in the Democratic Republic of Congo. He is the only boy of eight living children in his family. In 1996, war broke out in eastern Congo. As a fifteen-year-old, he witnessed the merciless killing of friends, neighbours and family. He managed to reunite with his family and lived five years in Nyarugusu refugee camp (Tanzania) where his family still lives. Msenwa was fortunate to complete his high school at Institut de l'Amitie in Nyarugusu refugee camp in 2000 before returning to DR Congo to promote peace and reconciliation among his people. He survived further atrocities and became a refugee living in both Kenya and Burundi.

While in Kenya, Msenwa enrolled at Hope Africa University to study Social Work, yet had no funds to support his education. A year later in 2004, the school was moved to Burundi and he faced further financial challenges. He prayed and trusted God for the means to continue studying. Through the sponsorship of an anonymous donor from the United States, he completed his undergraduate degree in 2007. Msenwa returned to Kenya in 2009 as a refugee and was blessed to be sponsored to immigrate to Canada by the FreeWay Free Methodist Church. While waiting to immigrate, through the support of an anonymous donor from Canada, Msenwa completed a Master of Leadership and Business from Pan Africa Christian University in Kenya. Upon arrival in Canada, Msenwa completed a Master of Social Work at the University of Waterloo.

Through perseverance and determination, Msenwa has emerged as a Social Worker who uses his lived experience to empower others. He has practiced social work in Africa and as a bilingual senior Social Worker at the Hincks-Dellcrest Centre in Toronto providing therapy to diverse children and families and currently as a bilingual Social Worker in the Greater Toronto Area where he lives with his wife Miriam. He is particularly interested in how policies affect the practice of macro social work to facilitate trauma-healing and migration.

Through this memoir, Msenwa aims to raise awareness about the needs of his people in Nyarugusu refugee camp and DR Congo. He is a registered Social Worker and the founder of the Msenwa Foundation, a non-profit organization that provides various supports, including educational assistance to Congolese in DR Congo and Nyarugusu refugee camp. He delivers inspirational and motivational keynotes and workshops. Msenwa speaks to universities, churches, corporate and non-profit organizations around the world. For further information about his presentations to associations and conferences or to book him for an event, contact the author at stillwithusmemoir@gmail.com or visit www.msenwafoundation.com.

CPSIA information can be obtained
at www.ICGtesting.com
Printed in the USA
LVOW12s1139050716

494984LV00005B/45/P

9 781926 798523